Wall Street

Mafia

Ben Skull (Alias)

AMZ Book Publishing
www.amzbookpublishings.com

Printed in the United States of America

Disclaimer:

This story is inspired by true events and real people. Some names, places, and details have been changed or blended to protect privacy and to tell the story the way it deserves to be told. Parts of what you'll read come straight from real experiences and records; other parts have been dramatized, condensed, or reimagined for storytelling purposes. Conversations and scenes have been recreated to capture the truth of what happened, even if not every word was said exactly that way. The author has done his best to tell it as honestly and fearlessly as possible. Any resemblance to actual persons, living or dead, beyond those intentionally included, is purely coincidental.

Dedication

Dedicated to my amazing wife, Ruth and my boys, Ethan, Benji, Brayden, Bradley, and Bryson.

I would also like to dedicate it to Michelle, Greyson and Ryder.

In memory of Evan B.

Acknowledgment

I want to give a special shout-out to my boss, H, who pulled me out of the gutter and gave me a shot at SLS Group in Utah. You changed my life by opening that door.

I also want to acknowledge Uncle Les, Dick and Jenny Johnson, Mama Maureen, and Papa, who all helped save me as a child. Dick and Jenny took me in when I was a young boy and taught me right from wrong, while Mama Maureen was my first foster mother who gave me stability when I needed it most.

And to my buddy, G, who trained me day in and day out, turning me into a polished ninja on Wall Street.

About the Author

Born in England and raised as a foster kid shuttling between two worlds, I've turned life's challenges into stepping stones for success. For 26 years, I've navigated the highs and lows of the stock market, building a career defined by resilience and savvy financial insight. In 2008, I embraced a new chapter as a proud US citizen, seizing opportunities with the same bold spirit that has driven me throughout my journey. My entrepreneurial drive led me to establish a Jeep company—an endeavor my son Benji affectionately named Skullkrushers, reflecting our family's fierce determination and unique legacy. Alongside being a devoted father to five boys, I'm also blessed with the unwavering love and support of an amazing wife and mother to our family. This journey, marked by both challenges and triumphs, continues to inspire me to push boundaries and forge new paths.

Table of Contents

The Rise & Early Success

Chapter 1: Welcome to Wall Street—The First Hit of Power

When my son Ethan was born, I was homeless and living on a friend's couch. I worked hard, started my first firm, and within a month had a Mercedes and a three-bedroom condo in Pacific Beach overlooking the water.

The first time I made a six-figure trade in under a minute, I knew there was no going back. The adrenaline hit me harder, so much so that it could only be defined as more than excitement or exhilaration but pure, raw, electrifying power surging through my veins, sharp and relentless, swirling my heart into a frenzy. My fingers trembled not out of fear; rather, it was just from a sheer feeling of what I had just done. Watching those numbers climb, watching my bank account swell by the second—it was intoxicating.

It was almost like instinct that I placed the order, like how a street hustler calls a bluff by reading the room instead of the rulebook. My gut said the right move, and in this game, hesitation meant death. One second, I was in; the other, it traded. And then, BOOM. Six figures in my pocket in less than sixty seconds. My pulse thundered in my ears, but I could still feel it—the electricity of the room. The chaos around me: phones ringing non-stop, traders barking into their headsets, deals closing at a breakneck speed. The air smelled of burnt coffee, sweat, and money.

I was not one of those privileged kids with a trust fund who went to Ivy League colleges. I was not born of money; I did not have a father playing golf with hedge fund managers, nor did I have a mother who hosted charity galas with wives of investment bankers. I did not spend my childhood summers in the Hamptons or attend prep schools, with tuition paid in full even before I was born. The closest thing I got was better balls and instincts.

The market didn't want to know your family background— it wanted to know who was brave enough to act first. While the Ivy League types were sitting there with their costly diplomas, their finely honed risk calculations, and their textbook theory, I was already two steps ahead. They were thinking it through. They were hedging. They were looking for validation. I saw it— the pause in their eyes, the uncertainty seeping into the way they moved. Their fingers hovered over their keys, in wait, always waiting for the market to give them the nod to move. But the market doesn't pay for waiting. It punishes it. Before they blinked, I was in and out, making more in minutes than most made in a year.

They didn't get it. To them, it appeared to be foolishness. But to me, it was merely the hustle—the same animal instincts that kept me alive on the streets, the same instinctual sense that allowed me to sense an opportunity before anyone else had even a clue it existed. I didn't require their spreadsheets or their risk profiles. I could smell the cash before it reached the screen. That's how I made a few grand into millions—I worked the market like a street hustle. I wasn't just raking it in; I was building a rep.

The brokers, the traders, even the fellas upstairs—everyone knew my name. Some spoke it quietly in awe. Others spat it out like it was a dirty word. Those who despised me said I was irresponsible, a gambler with more luck than a brain. Those who respected me said I was a shark. But none of it mattered to me. I only wanted one thing. The numbers. And the numbers were always in my favor.

The money came fast, and I spent it even faster. Why wouldn't I? I was just in my twenties, earning the sort of money most could only fantasize about—money that didn't just open doors, it knocked them off their hinges. Private jets flew me to Panama, where I'd sip rum on the deck of a luxury villa overlooking the ocean, the warm Caribbean breeze mingling with the scent of expensive cigars. There were yacht parties in the Bahamas that lasted for days, a blur of music, tanned bodies, and top-shelf liquor flowing like water. I stayed in suites at the Ritz-Carlton, where the concierge addressed me by name and always made sure a bottle of Cristal was chilled and waiting in the room.

Unlike others, I had never bothered asking for the price of anything. The moment I desired something, I would buy it. Flying to different destinations was not a problem, as I would always fly first class wherever I desired to go. I would be sitting in the VIP booth of the hottest nightclub in the city while a $10,000 bottle of Dom Pérignon would grace the table, with models on each of my arms. My phone would buzz endlessly with stock alerts, messages coming from brokers, and calls from people who had to call me to make them wealthier. Music vibrated through my chest, the bass pumping like my very heartbeat.

The lights strobed across the faces of the people surrounding me—traders, dealers, playboys, socialites, sharks. The chatter ran together, just white noise to the true high—the thrill of the trade. Work and play? They weren't two different things for me—until that point, they were one and the same damn thing. And then there were women—strippers, escorts, socialites, even a few celebrities. They weren't with me out of love. They were there for cash. The access. The power. And I didn't care. Love was the last thing on my mind. I had everything—or so I thought. But as I was drowning in excess, I was also drawing attention—the wrong kind of attention. And in this world, that kind of attention always comes with a price.

The bigger my trades got, the more dangerous the people I met. Wall Street wasn't just about stocks; it was about power. And power always comes with a price. Eventually, the suits and ties were no longer the only ones calling. The street sharks began to circle. And in this world, when sharks begin to circle, you learn to swim—or get eaten. I was not stupid. I knew that cash—real cash, the kind that made men legends or specters—didn't go in a direct line. It didn't lie securely in retirement accounts or hedge funds. It flowed in and out of places the SEC couldn't touch.

The real power existed in the background, in backroom deals, in things said over glasses of whiskey that cost more than a year's rent. And if you played long enough at the top, sooner or later, you were likely to meet men who were playing not for money, but for control. That's when the invitation came.

I met my first real gangster at a private poker game in New York—one of those invitation-only games where the bets were outrageous and the players weren't merely wealthy but influential. It wasn't in some cramped backroom in a crummy bar. This was penthouse luxury, the sort of joint where the doorman knew your name, where security wasn't a couple of bouncers but guys who looked like they came from the military. The sort of joint where threats shouted at the top of your lungs meant less than a whispered word. As soon as I walked in, I could sense it—the subtle thrum of power hanging in the air, heavy and unvoiced. A black-suited waiter poured a glass of whiskey into my hand before I even asked for one. Not whiskey—Louis XIII. A bottle of that costs more than most people make in a year.

The suite was dark, not to hide anything, but because men who resided at the top didn't need to be seen—they already had their hands on everything. The New York skyline glowed beyond the glass walls, a quiet reminder that money was the ruler of this city. The men in this room did not report to anyone—not the government, not the law, not even one another. The air was thick with the smell of leather armchairs, costly cigars, and old scotch. The quiet murmur of conversations, an occasional snap of a lighter, and the rustle of silk suits as men leaned forward to place their bets. No yelling, no outbursts.

Everything was controlled, precise, and deliberate. And then, naturally, there was the money. Piles of money on the felt table, neatly stacked in mounds that could have purchased whole buildings. Black and purple casino chips—$5,000, $25,000 bets—clinked as they were laid. The cards glided across the table with a smoothness that left no doubt: this wasn't a game. It was war. A location where reputations were made and broken. And where the wrong move could cost more than just money.

But it wasn't money that made this room unsafe. It was individuals. The guys at the table weren't mere traders—they were players. Money moguls. Real estate moguls. CEOs with politicians on their payroll. And then him. He wasn't some pseudo-tough guy, the type who tossed threats just to be taken seriously. No, this was a Montreal-made man, well entrenched in the mafia, and his presence alone was enough to command respect. He didn't have to demonstrate that he was dangerous—you could sense it. He wasn't boisterous. Didn't have to be. But when he spoke, the room quieted down. Men who dominated boardrooms leaned forward when he spoke. Bankers who typically played puppet masters themselves were reduced to being puppets. And for some reason, he liked me. Perhaps he saw something in me—the hunger, the hustle, the willingness to take risks. Perhaps he saw a younger version of himself. He leaned back in his chair, stirring a glass of whiskey in his hand, looking at me with sharp, knowing eyes.

"Kid, you remind me of me," he said finally, lighting a thick cigar. The flame flickered between us, casting shadows over his face. "You got the hunger. But hunger without control? That'll get you killed."

I should've listened. Instead, I laughed it off. Kept moving faster. Kept making bigger deals. Kept spending bigger money.

I thought I was untouchable.

I was wrong...

Chapter 2: Seventeen Grand

I started my own firm in 2005.

The new firm wasn't radically different from the last. It was just another squad of sharp suits playing the same Wall Street hustle, except with a bit more polish. I already knew the owner from my old firm. I remembered seeing him pull up in a red Ferrari with my old boss, just as they were heading into a meeting with the SEC. They looked like kings, oozing confidence. I watched them roll in and thought to myself, *Damn, that guy is a f*** pimp.*

So when I decided to give finance one last shot, I figured I might as well work under someone who clearly knew how to move money. I joined his firm and hit the ground running.

Not long after, I closed the biggest deal of my career—helping move a stock that had just received FDA approval. The price exploded. The owner of the firm had loaded up heavily on the stock before the announcement; he knew it had potential, but it was my hustle that turned potential into payoff. I executed the trade. When that FDA approval hit and the stock exploded, his position skyrocketed in value. Practically overnight, I made the guy a fortune. There were millions in gains, all flowing straight into his account. I did the legwork. I made the call. And he walked away with enough profit to buy another Ferrari.

I should've been set. This was supposed to be my payday.

Then my check came in: *seventeen thousand dollars.*

Seventeen grand for a deal that made this guy a fortune. I stared at that check, and it felt like a punch to the gut. It wasn't just a small commission cut, it was theft. And to make it worse, I had literally helped fund his bar in Del Mar, supporting his side ventures while he quietly pocketed what should have been mine.

That was the final straw... my breaking point.

I was done building other people's empires. I wasn't just chasing money anymore but was on a mission to do it the right way. I had seen firsthand just how insanely profitable this business could be, but I also knew, deep down, that you didn't have to cut throats or burn bridges to win. There had to be a way to play the game with integrity and to build wealth without leaving a trail of broken trust behind you. The Wall Street world was crawling with sharks, but I was determined not to become one of them. If I was going to stay in the game, it was going to be on my terms.

Looking back, maybe that mindset started way earlier... long before Wall Street.

I was just two years old when I first came to America, too young to remember much of England. But when I returned at nine, I didn't go back home. I walked straight into the unknown. My grandmother had been my anchor and the only real sense of family I ever had. She was warm and kind in a world that often felt unstable. When breast cancer took her, it was like the last tether to anything safe or familiar had been severed. My mother didn't wait long. She made a decision, fast and final. One day, she dropped me off at a foster home in England and left. She gave me no explanation or any warning. There was not even a goodbye.

One moment, I was a kid with a life. The next, I was just another file in the system. Another forgotten name in a strange country, trying to make sense of why the people who were supposed to protect me had vanished without a trace.

Being the American kid in an English school was like walking around with a neon sign on my back. I didn't sound like them. I didn't look like I belonged. And in a place where conformity was currency, that made me an outsider from day one. It didn't take long before a group of kids decided to test me, thinking I was an easy target. What they didn't know was that I came with a piece of quiet protection. It was a gift from my grandfather. He gave me a protractor shaped like a pirate ship. Most kids saw it as a school supply. I saw it as a reminder that sometimes, survival means being prepared for the unexpected.

One day, they surrounded me, taunting, pushing and daring me to fold. But I didn't fold. I wasn't about to let a pack of schoolyard bullies decide who I was or where I belonged. I pulled out the retractor and fought back. I stabbed each of them in the arms, right through their white school shirts. I remember the blood soaking into the fabric and the cries that followed. I got sent to the principal's office, fully expecting to be expelled or worse. But they let me go. They knew my situation.

That moment didn't just teach me how to fight back. It taught me not to let anyone else write my story. Not kids in a schoolyard. Not firm owners in Ferraris. Not anyone.

So, I started my own firm.

From day one, I ran my firm clean with no shady deals, no backdoor commissions, no schemes dressed up as strategy. Just straight, honest business. I built my reputation on trust, and over time, I became known as one of the best in investor relations. Years after leaving the industry, my name still carried weight. You may ask "Why?" Because people knew I never ripped anyone off.

Did I get ripped off along the way? Absolutely. More times than I can count. But I could sleep at night knowing I didn't have to look over my shoulder. No feds chasing me, no subpoenas landing on my doorstep and no wiretaps replaying my words. Just the quiet satisfaction of building something, with a clear conscience and a clear mind.

Today, I'm a husband and a father of five boys. That's my empire. That's the legacy I care about, not just the money I made, but the way I made it. Because when it's all said and done, your name and your word—that's worth more than any deal.

Chapter 3: Brotherhood and the Code

I was in my twenties when I first met Big S, the president of the Hells Angels San Diego chapter. He was my neighbor, and at first, our relationship was simple—just nods in passing. But over time, we became close. He had a wife, two sons, and a presence that commanded respect without ever asking for it. Despite his role in one of the most feared motorcycle clubs in the world, he was grounded. Family came first when he wasn't handling club business.

Back then, I was running Powerhouse Gym in Pacific Beach, right there on the sand, overlooking the ocean. But this wasn't one of those polished, corporate fitness chains with scented towels and smoothie bars. This was a real gym. There were no gimmicks and no sales pitches. Just steel and sweat.

I let Big S and his brothers train there for free. It wasn't about money. It was about respect. These were men who lived by a different code, one most people wouldn't understand, but I did. And they knew it. That's why they accepted me.

I wasn't a patch-holder, but in that world, I didn't need one. I was embraced as a brother. For a long time, I even thought about prospecting for them. That's how deep the bond was. I loved those guys—the brotherhood, the structure, the loyalty. There was something powerful about the sense of family they shared. The guys were incredibly solid and loyal. I admired their strength, their code, and the way they carried themselves. They respected me, too, and that meant everything.

Even though I never took the step to officially join, my love for the club has never faded. I've been a supporter for over twenty-seven years, and that loyalty still runs deep. I don't talk to them as often these days, but whenever we do see each other, it's like no time has passed.

Hanging around the club, you see things no movie or documentary could ever fully capture. There was an electricity in the air, charged with danger, loyalty, and an eerie kind of grace. The club was never meant for the weak. It was built for men who had proven themselves, who had earned their place through loyalty, strength, and resilience. Although I never wore a patch, I was welcomed in a way that few civilians ever were.

Then came the loss. One of my closest friends in the club, a brother, passed away. It hit hard. Even though I wasn't a member of the club, I still showed up to his funeral. I was the only civilian there, and that meant something. I stood quietly off to the side, dressed in black, observing as line after line of patched brothers took their places in solemn silence. There was no weeping or long-winded speeches.

When the service ended, a few of the older members approached me. They nodded and shook my hand. Their expressions were serious but respectful. In those brief gestures, I felt something I hadn't expected: acceptance.

That day, I didn't earn their respect through grand gestures or long-standing titles. I earned it by simply showing up. And in doing so, I had crossed an invisible line—one that separates outsiders from those who are quietly, undeniably part of the brotherhood.

**

The club didn't exist in a vacuum. It had enemies. The war with the Mongols in the desert was legendary. What started in the sand didn't stay there. It spilled into cities and streets, into neighborhoods and local businesses.

Big S owned a tattoo shop in Pacific Beach. One afternoon, in broad daylight, someone walked in and put a .45 to his stomach. There was no warning or words. He just pulled the trigger.

I still remember the moment I got the call. On the other end of the line was chaos. There was shouting and panic. Big S was rushed to the hospital, barely hanging on. His life was slipping through the cracks. Incidents like that don't make headlines the way they should. To the public, it was just another shooting in San Diego. Another nameless victim with so-called "gang ties." But to us, it was so much more. It was a direct hit. It was war. Whether it was payback, a warning, or just years of bad blood finally catching up with him, we didn't know. All we knew was that it was real, and it cut deep. When you live it, even as a friend, you might feel every bullet, every bruise, and every loss.

In my thirties, I started traveling up to Vancouver regularly, probably once a month for meetings. Life was different, but in many ways, it was the same. During those trips, I reconnected with a few of the Hells Angels brothers up there. Just like before, we connected instantly. These men lived by the same code. And once again, I was accepted. We shared wild nights, crazy stories, gym sessions, and conversations.

Over time, life took us in different directions, but the memories stayed. Even now, I still talk to a few of the brothers from time to time. We follow each other on social media, shoot the occasional message. But that's about the extent of it.

The truth is, I preferred dealing with men from the street—wise guys and bikers. There was a sense of honor. If you made a deal, you honored it. If you crossed a line, you paid for it. That kind of integrity was absent in the world I came from professionally. Wall Street was a shark tank. The finance world was filled with suits who would stab you in the back, smile in your face, and shake your hand while they stole your life. I feel like the streets had more ethics than the boardroom ever did.

During those years, every Friday like clockwork, a new subpoena from the SEC or the Feds would land on my desk. It became part of my weekly routine. I'd get served, then head into their office and sit across from a room full of federal agents. Every time they asked a question, I gave the same response: "I plead the Fifth."

They came at me hard. Between five and seven federal subpoenas over the years. I never said anything because I never committed a crime. The Feds had a file on me about five inches thick. They had everything: aliases, websites, history. But they never had evidence of a crime. Because I never committed one.

I spent a fortune on legal fees. The stress was brutal. But I had an old-school lawyer who never flinched. He held the line, and we gave them nothing. I walked away clean every single time and never slipped. I never crossed the line and that's why my reputation remains rock solid. I was honest. I played it by the book. And I never broke.

Even the Feds respected that. We may have been on opposite sides of the table, but they were always professional. They were tough, yes. But respectful. They knew I was a man who chose to play with integrity.

Every time I had to meet with the government, that respect never changed. I kept it simple: name, date of birth, and nothing more. The men I called friends taught me that rule from the beginning: never talk to the Feds. Not under pressure, not for a deal, not ever.

I also knew the system better than most. The game of offshore brokers in Belize, Panama, Costa Rica, the Bahamas— shell companies, new firms popping up as fast as the Feds could shut them down. It was like a carnival of smoke and mirrors. When one went down, another would pop up in its place, on a new island or in a new foreign country, like clockwork. I watched it unfold from the sidelines, knowing exactly how it all worked, and knowing exactly when to stay out of it.

I've spent most of my career surrounded by chaos, danger, and temptation. But I never let it define me. I never let it pull me under. I survived because I knew who I was, and more importantly, who I wasn't. I knew my line, and I never crossed it. In a world where loyalty is rare and respect is often faked, I earned mine the old-fashioned way—by showing up, by standing firm, and by never breaking my word.

That's the code I live by.

And maybe that's why I'm still standing.

Chapter 4: The One

By the early 2000s, our Fridays had a rhythm. After a long week at Powerhouse Gym, every Friday, like clockwork, my crew and I would head next door to Hooters—beers in hand, wings on deck, loud laughs, louder stories. It was tradition.

And every Friday, we had the same waitress.

She was this stunning Latina with blonde highlights, glowing skin, and eyes that pulled you in like a tide. She was always smiling, always cool under pressure. She had a boyfriend, but that didn't matter. Not in the way you'd think. I wasn't trying to be disrespectful. I just couldn't ignore the pull. There was something about her energy; it felt real, electric, and calm all at once. She had this way of making you feel seen without trying. And me? I'd just sit there, drink in hand, watching her move through that place like she owned it. Quietly thinking, *Damn... she's the one.*

But I never crossed the line. I never made a move. I just enjoyed the moment. Fridays were ours in this small, unspoken way.

Then one day, she was gone. A few months later, I walked into a barbershop, and there she was. Clippers in hand, cutting hair. She'd traded the Hooters shorts for a barber's cape, and just like that, our worlds collided again. She became my barber, and from that day on, she stayed in my life. For over twenty years, she's been the one behind the chair, cutting my hair while listening to all the madness that came with me. I told her *everything.* The wild nights, the insane stories, the hookers, the cash, the chaos. And she never flinched. Never judged. She'd just laugh, shake her head, and keep cutting. There's something very interesting about that kind of acceptance, when someone sees all the grime and doesn't look away.

I'd find excuses just to see her. And yeah, maybe I tried to show her my world in little ways. Every time I got a new car—and there were a lot of them—a Porsche, a Range Rover, an Aston, a Benz—I'd show up, flash the keys, and take her out to lunch. It became our thing. A new car meant a new lunch date. I never said it out loud, but yeah, I was trying to impress her. Showing her what I'd built, what I was about. A part of me was saying, *Look at the life I can give you.*

And deep down? I already knew she was the one. I knew it before she ever moved in. But when she finally did, everything changed.

One night, everything hit the wall. The cops had raided my house—illegally, by the way. I'll talk about this in detail later but that was the day she asked me *the question*. She was sitting across from me with her eyes filled with tears. She looked at me like she didn't even know who I was anymore.

"What do you really do for a living?"

Stacks of cash, nonstop hustle, always on the move, always flexing. She saw it all. She wasn't stupid—she knew this life came with shadows and that there was more to the story.

I looked her in the eyes and gave her the only answer I could give.

"I do stocks."

And I did. But that wasn't the whole story. Not the world she was seeing. I had assistants, young college girls, and hot nannies around the house. My son had everything—trips, toys, the best of the best. From the outside, it looked like a dream. But inside? It was a firestorm. Flashy, reckless, and dangerous.

Still, she stayed through it all. Through every moment of madness. Through every sideways glance and shady situation. She didn't just become my girl. She became my anchor. My ride-or-die.

She never ran, never looked the other way. Even when things didn't make sense—even when the world around us was filled with noise, pressure, and uncertainty—she stayed grounded. Maybe she didn't always understand every situation I was involved in, but she always understood me. And that made all the difference to me.

Today, we are blessed with four boys together, and watching her with them has only deepened my respect and love for her. She is an extraordinary mother—loving, strong, patient, and fiercely devoted. What amazes me even more is the way she has embraced my oldest son, who is now twenty-two, with the same level of care and love. To him, and to all five of my boys, she is a role model. They admire her, they respect her, and they love her deeply.

She is one of a kind. Loyal beyond words. She has had my back through every high and every low. In our world, where trust is rare and loyalty even rarer, she has been my constant. She is not just the heart of our family. She is our queen.

And in that truth, I found my answer. That is how I knew she was the one.

Chapter 5: The Kind of Loyalty You Can't Buy

If you knew us back then, you'd know better than to mess with me and E. We were a dangerous mix. We weren't reckless or cruel—we just never backed down. We took care of our own, stood our ground, didn't bluff, and made it clear where the lines were drawn. That kind of confidence only comes when you know someone has your back without question. And E? He always had mine.

E was a real estate mogul and an OG from Sacramento, where we grew up in a town called Folsom. One of the wildest nights we ever had started, like too many of them, with a fight. I can't even remember what sparked it, but I ended up with my forehead split wide open. Blood was pouring down my face like a busted faucet. Most people would've freaked out and called 911 or rushed to the hospital, wrapped me in towels. But not E. He looked at me, shook his head like I'd just spilled a drink, and calmly pulled out a tube of super glue.

"Hold still," he said, like he was fixing a cracked mug instead of sealing up a gash on my skull. He smeared the glue across the wound, let it dry, and nodded. "Good as new." That was E—no panic, no theatrics, just action. Like it was Tuesday.

But that wasn't even the craziest night.

We were on the freeway: me, my brother Casey, and E tailing us in his S-Class. I was in the passenger seat of my Aston Martin, just cruising, nothing out of the ordinary and Casey was driving the car. Then, out of nowhere, this cracked-out lunatic in a beat-up piece of junk swerved and tried to ram us off the road. There was no reason. Just full-throttle insanity.

Big mistake.

We were not the kind of men to let that slide. We boxed him in and forced him into a dead-end cul-de-sac. I stepped out of the car with my shotgun in hand and walked straight up to his driver's window. The second he saw me and that barrel in my hand, he froze like a deer in headlights. I leaned in, looked him dead in the eye, and said, calm as anything, "You know you f*** up, right?"

He nodded so fast it looked like his neck might snap. I did not have to say another word. The message had been delivered. We left him there, sitting in silence, completely rattled, probably rethinking every bad decision that brought him to that moment.

Then there was the rental property incident. E owned the place, but some Mexican gangbangers had moved in illegally and refused to leave. He called the cops, but they gave him the runaround. "It'll take time," they said. E didn't have time. He didn't wait on systems. He called me.

We rolled up in bulletproof vests with a bag of hardware in the back seat. Kicking in the door wasn't the hard part. The real moment came when they saw our eyes and realized we weren't there to negotiate. While we were there, we called the police, a helicopter circled, and the street was blocked off.

We laid it out plain: leave now, or stay and find out what happens next. A few firm words, a flash of firepower, and suddenly, they remembered they had somewhere else to be. They packed up and left without a fight. We fired no shots and there were no shouts. Just respect.

We were always ready. Ready to ride, ready to fight, ready to bleed if we had to. We didn't look for trouble, but if it knocked, we answered. Together, we were the kind of problem people didn't want.

***

In early 2008, when I first began dating my wife, we lived the kind of life that came with youth and disposable income. We went out often. We hit clubs, had limousines, sat at VIP tables, and ordered bottle service without a second thought. I had money back then, and when you have it, you spend it. That was the norm.

One night, one of my wife's friends came into town. Her husband was a guy I had met a few times before. He seemed like a good dude, at least that's what I thought at the time. We got along easily. We had drinks together and laughed, and even though we weren't close, I considered him a friend. In those days, if we partied together and spent money together, that was enough to call someone your brother.

That night turned chaotic. The drinks kept coming, and soon everything blurred together—shots, music, laughter, and eventually, a blackout.

My boy E was with me. At some point during the night, my wife's friend went missing. Just vanished from the group. After a while, we spotted her walking down the street, holding onto some random guy. Her husband turned to me and said, "Hey, make sure my wife doesn't do anything stupid."

I didn't pause. I didn't think it through. I reached into my pocket, pulled out my Audi key (the kind with the metal blade that flips out) and stabbed the man in the neck. Not once or twice but six times.

There was blood everywhere. The scene was something out of a nightmare.

We didn't wait around. E and I left immediately and ended up at his apartment. I was still covered in blood. We poured hydrogen peroxide over my clothes and skin, trying to erase the evidence. We even laughed about it, like it was laundry, not a near-death mistake. That was our dynamic. E never panicked. He never asked why. He just helped clean me up, like it was another crazy night in a string of many. He was my brother.

At the time, it felt like a story I would tell years later, not something that would follow me.

But the next morning, reality came crashing in.

Thankfully, the man I stabbed survived. He had been released from the hospital and knew exactly who I was. Even worse, I knew him too. I had worked security at his club once. He was a good person, someone I had no beef with him. And yet, because of a split-second decision and some misplaced sense of loyalty to a guy I barely knew, I had nearly ended his life.

Then came the phone call.

He told me he wanted to talk. If I didn't agree, he would go to the police. I didn't argue or lie. I called him immediately, apologized, and told him the truth: I had no memory of what happened. I didn't make excuses and simply took responsibility. I felt horrible. As a gesture of remorse, I paid for a luxury spa weekend getaway for him and his wife at La Costa. It didn't make up for what I had done, but it was something.

He didn't press charges. I'll never know exactly why. Maybe he was afraid. Maybe he just wanted to move on. Either way, that moment changed something in me.

A few months later, I was flying to Las Vegas with a friend, Sandman. I'll tell you more about him later. Anyways, we were heading out for a mix of business and fun. As I settled into my seat on the plane, someone boarded and took the seat right in front of me. Guess who it was?

The man I stabbed.

He looked right at me. Neither of us said a word. I sat there, frozen, unsure of whether he was going to start something or let it go. I leaned over to Sandman and quietly explained what had happened months earlier. We both laughed nervously, but I couldn't shake the weight of that moment.

Looking back now, I realize the truth: I nearly destroyed a man and seriously hurt him over a false sense of brotherhood... fake loyalty. I barely knew the person I had acted for, and when everything went sideways, he didn't hesitate to throw me under the bus. He gave up on me. The loyalty I showed him wasn't returned.

Lesson learned: don't do stupid shit for people you think are loyal to you. Most of the time, they're not

But E was different.

He stood beside me that night. He didn't question me. He didn't flinch. He didn't leave. That was the kind of friend he was. Through everything—good, bad, wild—he stood beside me. And I stood beside him.

He's gone now. And my world feels like it's missing a piece.

Rest easy, E. I'll never forget you.

Chapter 6: The Sandman

In our world, everyone had a code name. Not just for secrecy but maybe also as a badge of honor, a symbol of who you were beneath the surface. I'll call him Sandman in these pages. I think that name fits him better. He wasn't loud or explosive. He moved with precision and a kind of power you didn't see until it was too late.

Sandman's story stayed with me. He grew up in Eastern Europe but carried the fire of a Mexican-American kid who had seen too much of the streets in East L.A. You didn't forget a guy like him. He was raw and someone you can't help but respect. He hadn't inherited wealth. There was no trust fund or backdoor deal waiting for him. Like me, he clawed his way up, step by step, through grit and obsession.

His parents were gangbangers. That could have been the end of his story. But he broke the cycle. He chose a different path that took everything you had and offered nothing back unless you took it for yourself. He became a force in the financial game. Not a name on a business card, but a name people whispered when the stakes got high.

The first time we met, the connection was instant. We spoke the same language: risk, numbers, and that deep hunger for more. I brought him a flood of accounts. Together, we built something that most people only dream about. In the early days, it was all hustle—sunrises we never saw because we were still at our desks, and sunsets we missed because we were still closing deals.

It worked. It worked like wildfire. We were always looking for the next big opportunity and traveling across cities like kings without thrones. Vegas, Miami, New York, Tulum, the islands. Wherever we went, the rooms opened up. Private jets, high-stakes poker games, suites that stretched like mansions in the sky. We drank the kind of whiskey you can't pronounce and partied with the kind of people you only see on magazine covers. Cash poured in, and every day felt like a nonstop surge of adrenaline.

There was a time when we believed we had cracked the code. Every deal felt like a success, and every dollar only made us push harder. But if you stay in the fire too long, it starts to burn. And eventually, even the Sandman has to wake up.

When I first met Sandman, he didn't look the part. He wore a Tommy Bahama shirt and a pair of Skechers that screamed clearance rack. We were headed to the Bahamas for a business trip, and the moment we got to the hotel, I grabbed those damn shoes and tossed them across the suite.

He looked at me, half amused and half annoyed. "What the hell are you doing?" he asked.

"Upgrading you," I said, dead serious.

Back then, I was all Gucci and Louis Vuitton, from my sunglasses to my cufflinks. Sandman got the message. After that trip, the transformation began. Gucci loafers. LV jackets. A watch on his wrist that cost more than most people's first car.

I looked at him one night and said, "You're welcome, buddy."

He laughed, but I could tell he liked who he was becoming.

At first, it was fun to watch. The kid from East L.A. was evolving. But it didn't stop there. Something changed in him. The hustle wasn't just about winning anymore. It became about domination. About control. About power.

The Sandman I knew was always ambitious. But now there was an edge. He stopped caring how he made money. He started cutting corners, bending rules, playing games with clients' accounts that didn't sit right with me.

At first, I let it go. We were making too much money. Private jets, luxury suites, and an endless stream of wins that I didn't question the details. But eventually, I had to. The numbers started getting weird. Clients were getting burned. Documents weren't matching. Whispers started floating around the industry.

As Sandman's empire grew, so did his appetite. His deals got riskier. His circles darker. I saw him one night at a club in Miami with a guy I didn't recognize. Everything about the man felt wrong—his stare, his silence, the way he watched the room.

I pulled Sandman aside and said, "I don't trust that guy. Stay away from him."

He brushed it off like I was being paranoid. But I knew that look in his eye. The hunger had overtaken the discipline. And just like that, the bond we had started to loosen. We weren't celebrating wins together anymore. We weren't taking trips. We weren't talking like we used to. And it stung, because Sandman and I had gone to war with the Russians in L.A. before. We'd been brothers in arms. Or at least, that's what I believed.

But money has a way of turning the blade sideways. It doesn't just change your life. It changes your loyalty.

I remember a conversation we had. We were in a penthouse at the Fontainebleau in Miami, sitting out on the balcony, staring at the Atlantic. I tried to pull him back.

"Man," I said, "you're playing with fire."

He grinned, lifted his glass, and said, "You think they'll catch me? I'm too smart for that."

That was the moment I knew I had to get out. He was too far gone.

Still, a part of me hoped he'd come around. So I sent him a couple of clients. He didn't even say thank you. He looked at the files, then looked at me like I'd insulted him.

"Why you bringing me this dog shit?" he snapped.

And just like that, I knew we weren't on the same team anymore. At the time, I remember thinking, *F*** you, bro.* I didn't say it out loud, but the words rang clear in my mind. He'd looked down on the business I brought him. Acted like he was too good for it. Too sharp. Too clean. But looking back, I see the truth now—that was God watching my back.

If Sandman had said yes to those deals, I might have gone down with him. In the government's eyes, guilt by association is enough. They don't care who signed what. If your name is anywhere near the wreckage, you go down too.

I handed him a few clients, legitimate ones. But he turned his nose up like I was insulting him. At the time, it pissed me off. Now, I'm thankful. That rejection was a blessing in disguise.

I started stepping back, keeping my distance. Something about the way he moved just didn't sit right anymore. And then it all started falling apart.

The Feds had been watching. Quietly and patiently but in a calculated manner. They raided his office while we were in Vegas celebrating his birthday. The weekend turned into disaster. That was the first crack in the illusion, more like the beginning of the end of Sandman.

After that, I backed away for good. Sandman was gone, replaced by someone I didn't recognize. Obsessed with power, drunk on status. I still loved making money, but I'd always kept one foot on solid ground, at least most of the time. He didn't. He'd gone off the deep end.

Then came the airport bust.

They caught him. It was a house arrest. It should have been a wake-up call, but instead of slowing down, he got desperate. Reached out to the same guy I warned him about. He wanted a fake passport. A Ukrainian one. He was planning to disappear.

What Sandman didn't know was that the guy was working for the Feds. It was a setup from the beginning. They let him dig his own grave, then handed him the shovel.

Meanwhile, a friend of mine from high school was doing some renovations at Sandman's oceanfront mansion in La Jolla. This place was unreal—$10 million estate right on the water. Glass walls, an infinity pool that looked like it spilled right into the Pacific, smart-home everything. But Sandman already knew he'd have to sell it. He'd burn through every asset just to stay out of prison.

And that day, while my buddy was patching drywall or fixing lighting or something, FBI agents came swarming out from the trees. From the bushes. Like ghosts in the garden. They surrounded the place and took him down. Final arrest. No more bail. No more running.

I've seen it happen more times than I can count. Money is like a drug. At first, you're in control. You feel powerful. Alive. Unstoppable. But then it starts whispering to you. Telling you you're different. Telling you the rules don't apply. That you're smarter than the rest. That you'll never get caught.

Sandman believed that lie.

And that's the thing about lies: they don't just destroy you. They destroy everything you touch. One day he was closing million-dollar deals and the next, he was standing in front of a federal judge, listening to a sentence that would take five years of his life.

When I heard the news, I can't say I was shocked. Saddened, yes. We had history. We built something together. There was a time when we were making good cash. But eventually, he let greed take the wheel. He forgot the one rule that matters more than any other in this game: make your money, but never let your money make you.

That's the difference between players who survive and those who get devoured whole.

Oddly enough, getting cut out of the business was one of the best things that ever happened to me. If he hadn't pushed me away, I never would have built Skullkrushers. And if I had stayed in his orbit, there's a good chance I would've ended up in the cell right next to him.

I'll never work with him again. That chapter is closed. Permanently.

I've been in this game for over twenty-five years. I've seen what money can do to people. How it seduces, how it blinds, how it turns smart men reckless and loyal friends into strangers. I've watched ambition rot into obsession. I've watched greed eat people alive.

And if there's one thing I know, it's this: When you chase the wrong things, they always catch you in the end.

Sandman thought he could outrun the consequences. But when the walls finally closed in, he found himself in a place money couldn't protect him.

Brooklyn jail.

Chapter 7: The Fall of the Hockey Player

He was the kind of guy you'd take one look at and underestimate—until you realized he was worth a billion dollars. The Canuck. A former hockey player, a six-foot-tall white man Canadian through and through. But instead of spending his days as a retired athlete, he built something massive—an offshore brokerage firm that became the go-to spot for anyone moving serious money. And by "anyone," I mean everyone.

The thing ran so hot, so clean, and so efficiently that it became one of the most valuable operations in the game. The Canuck had built it from the ground up. He never traded a single stock himself, never played games with the numbers—just kept the machine running. And it ran so well that before long, the valuation was sitting comfortably north of a billion. It wasn't just a business; it was an institution. Everybody who mattered in that world touched it in some way.

And the guy behind it? Man, he was a good dude. One of the best. If you ever got to know him, you'd see it instantly—warm, loyal, the kind of guy who'd give you the shirt off his back. But if you just saw him walking down the street, you'd probably think, *Who the hell is this guy?* Tall, unassuming, didn't carry himself like a billionaire. No flash, no arrogance—just a sharp mind and a quiet confidence.

He had a big house up in Huntington Beach, just a short walk from the ocean. It was the kind of setup that made you stop and take a deep breath. He also bought himself an airline jet just because he could. He was loving life, living life. His family included of two beautiful little girls and a blonde wife straight out of a dream. He had everything they could ever need. It should've been perfect.

But the Feds don't like perfect.

Especially not when you're a former hockey player turned financial mastermind running a billion-dollar offshore firm they can't touch. And if there's one thing about the Feds, it's that when they want their pound of flesh, they take it. Didn't matter that he never did anything wrong. Didn't matter that he wasn't out there playing games or screwing people over. They needed someone to burn, and he was a high-profile guy sitting in their crosshairs.

The Canuck had started his own airline with three private jets worth $20–30 million each, which the feds later seized.

Eight years.

That's what they took from him—eight years behind bars for what? For running a business people chose to use? For being successful? He never flipped. Never snitched. Never tried to buy his way out with someone else's blood. He did his time like a man, missing his daughters' childhoods, missing everything he'd built his life for. The system didn't just take his money—it took moments he could never get back.

Now he's back in Vancouver, free but changed. A little older, a little wiser, but still one of the humblest guys in the business. He doesn't bitch, doesn't complain, just moves forward. Because that's the kind of guy he is. The Feds took their pound of flesh, but they didn't break him.

That's our justice system—burn the good ones while the crooks keep rolling.

Chapter 8: Brooklyn Jail

Both the Canuck and Sandman were initially sent to the Brooklyn jail.

The first night in Brooklyn Jail didn't feel real. The Canuck barely slept that night.

He lay on the top bunk, arms crossed over his chest, eyes open wide, listening to the violent orchestra of prison life play out around him. Somewhere down the tier, a man screamed, cut off by the sharp clang of a cell door slamming shut. The mattress beneath him was thin as a paper towel with metal springs that groaned every time he shifted. The toilet in the corner dripped in irregular intervals, as if mocking him with each hollow splash.

Just some nights ago, he'd been sipping coffee in a sky-high suite. Now, he was just another inmate, watching cockroaches crawl across the floor.

It wasn't the jail that unsettled him... it was the unit they threw him into.

They didn't assign him to a pod filled with white-collar criminals, the ones who talked like lawyers and traded legal advice for ramen packs. No. They threw him into a war zone. His cellblock was filled with killers and drug lords. It was a section where alliances meant survival and staring too long meant you were picking a fight.

He stood out immediately as he was the only white guy there.

Six-foot-five, broad frame, too well-fed and too well-groomed. He had the look of a man who'd made his fortune legally, or at least clean enough to fake it. In this place, none of that mattered. Size meant nothing – reputation did. Even wealth was worthless unless you could use it to buy loyalty. And Sandman had nothing to trade.

He kept to himself the first day. He knew how to read people, and it was obvious they were watching. Not out of curiosity but calculation. They were waiting to see how he'd handle pressure. How he'd carry himself. If he flinched, it was over.

"Yo, big man!" someone called out from across the yard.

He turned toward the voice and saw a cluster of men— Mexican mafia by the look of them. Their bodies were covered in tattoos and their eyes were locked onto him with a mix of curiosity and challenge.

"You got your paperwork?" one of them asked.

He understood immediately. In prison, everything hinged on your charges. If you were inside for anything shady, especially sex crimes or ratting someone out, you became a target fast.

Keeping his tone calm and even, Sandman replied, "I'm in here over some finance crap case."

The men exchanged glances. One of them cracked a grin.

"Wrong unit, Wall Street," he said.

He already knew that. No Kidding.

***

The guards watched the Canuck closely, not out of concern but amusement. They were the ones who had placed him here, knowing full well the blood games that played out in this block. They didn't help and it seemed like they treated him like he was part of a show. The fights weren't official, but everyone knew they were organized.

One afternoon, a correctional officer opened his cell door and told him he had a "matchup." No explanation. No warning. No choice.

He was led into a grim, echoing room that had been turned into a makeshift fight pit. A crowd of inmates circled around, jeering, shouting, placing bets with manic energy.

Across from him stood his opponent. He was a gang enforcer with a face like stone, scars across his knuckles, and a body carved from muscle. He looked like he'd been built for violence.

The fight didn't last long.

He slipped past the first punch, instinct and muscle memory kicking in. This wasn't some barroom scuffle or hockey fight. There were no referees here. No rules. No timeouts. He had to finish it before it dragged on.

And he did.

A sharp right hook landed clean across the man's jaw, making him stumble. Without pause, he drove a body shot into his ribs, followed by another. They were fast, relentless strikes that dropped the enforcer to the ground.

Silence swept through the room.

Then the noise exploded: shouts, whistles, laughter. The crowd loved it. So did the guards.

One of them leaned against the doorway and smirked. "Not bad."

That was when the truth settled in his chest. This wasn't about a single fight. It wasn't about survival. It was about control. And he understood now… they had no plans to stop.

They made him fight again some days later. And again after that.

The fights kept coming. Every few days, they sent in someone new looking to make a name for himself, or just trying to survive. He kept winning, and that quickly became a problem.

The victories came too easily. His reflexes were sharp, and he knew how to move. He wasn't fighting to prove anything. He was fighting because there was no other choice. But one afternoon, everything changed.

During a fight, he swung hard—too hard. His fist connected with the side of the other man's skull, and the moment it landed, he felt it. A sickening crunch shot up his arm, followed by a blinding flash of pain.

His hand was broken. He didn't need a doctor to tell him.

He went to the guards, holding his swollen hand, expecting they'd call medical or at least take him off rotation. Instead, they laughed.

"You still got another one, don't you?" one of them said with a smirk.

And just like that, the fights continued. They forced him into the ring with a shattered hand. Every punch sent a wave of pain through his body. But opting out wasn't an option. Refuse, and he'd end up the one being beaten or maybe worse. So he kept swinging. Kept bleeding. Kept surviving.

The Canuck's a free man now, back in Canada with his wife and two girls, restarting his life.

***

As the days passed, the stories in the prison grew darker. One inmate, a cartel enforcer, told the Sandman about a guy who got decapitated over a gang feud. They found the body in the shower and the head dumped in another unit like a trophy.

Days blurred into weeks and weeks dragged into months.

Brooklyn Jail didn't kill you quickly... it wore you down, piece by piece. It wasn't the violence that broke him, or even the cruelty of the guards. It was the slow erosion of everything human. The isolation. The noise. The constant sense of being trapped under the weight of a life that no longer belonged to him. It felt like being buried alive, inch by inch.

Sandman had always been a fighter in every hard moment life threw his way. But this was something else entirely. There was no game plan here, no clever move to turn the tide. Survival wasn't about smarts. It was about endurance.

And in the world outside prison, life had moved on without him. And no one seemed to give a damn.

His attorney came once a week, always at the same time, always wearing the same polished suit that looked like it belonged in a high-rise office—not in a room surrounded by cold cement walls and flickering fluorescent lights. The contrast was almost comical. On one side of the glass: clean lines, crisp cuffs, a silk tie. On the other: orange fabric, handcuffs, and air that smelled like disinfectant and metal.

During one of those visits, the lawyer slid a thin sheet of paper across the table.

"They want you to take a deal," he said quietly.

He didn't even look down. "What kind of deal?"

"Conspiracy to commit fraud," the lawyer replied. "If you plead guilty, they'll reduce the sentence to five years."

He let out a dry, bitter laugh and shook his head. "I'm not signing that."

The lawyer exhaled and rubbed his temples, clearly frustrated. "They don't care if you're guilty. They just want a conviction."

He didn't need the reminder. He understood all too well how the system worked. Guilt didn't matter, not when the government could hit you with enough charges to bury your future under paperwork and public opinion. Their strategy was simple: overwhelm, isolate, pressure. And eventually, people cracked.

They had already taken everything from him. His bank accounts were frozen. His brokerage firm was shut down. His home and assets were gone. They even seized his wife's car.

"They'll keep you in here as long as they need to," the lawyer warned. "You need to think long-term."

Long-term... Easy for him to say.

Outside these walls, his life was already in ruins. People had already made up their minds. His name was radioactive. His wife couldn't even walk the kids to school without getting side-eyed or whispered about.

And if he lost at trial? He knew what that meant. Decades behind bars.

If he refused to play along, they'd leave him here until he begged for a way out.

***

Word traveled fast inside. It always did.

One afternoon, while Sandman sat alone in the yard, a senior member of the Mexican Mafia approached and took the seat beside him. This wasn't one of the younger guys running errands or trying to prove something. This was someone with real authority. A shot caller. The kind of man who didn't need to raise his voice to be heard.

"You've got problems in here, Wall Street," the man said casually.

He didn't respond. The understatement didn't deserve one.

The gang leader lit a cigarette, inhaling slowly as he scanned the yard. His movements were unhurried and confident, like a predator that knew no one would dare challenge him.

"We can take care of that."

Still, Sandman stayed silent.

"If you roll with us," the man continued, flicking ash to the ground, "you're protected."

It wasn't phrased as a threat, but it wasn't a simple offer either. In prison, nothing was free. He knew exactly what this meant. Accept their protection, and he'd belong to them. That came with expectations, with loyalty; not the kind you gave willingly, but the kind you owed in blood.

He glanced at his knuckles. They were still swollen and throbbing from the last fight. Every punch he threw was a reminder of what survival looked like in here.

Was this what it came to? Becoming someone else just to stay alive?

He wasn't sure what frightened him more: the violence, or the possibility that he might say yes.

***

Later that night, Sandman got a rare call. It had been weeks since he'd heard anything from the outside.

His wife's voice crackled through the line. "Hey," she said gently. "How are you holding up?"

He leaned against the glass, gripping the receiver tight. "Living the dream," he muttered.

She didn't laugh. Then came the words that cut through him like a blade. "The kids keep asking why you're not home."

His chest tightened. He swallowed hard and forced himself to speak. "What did you tell them?"

"I told them that Daddy's fighting to come home," she replied.

He closed his eyes and inhaled slowly, trying to steady the chaos inside him.

He wanted to tell her that everything was fine, that he had things under control. But the truth sat heavy in his chest. He wasn't fine. And nothing was under control.

"I need you," she said in a low and fragile voice.

In that single moment, he felt something inside him change. And as Sandman lay on his bed that night, he stared at the ceiling and came to a quiet conclusion. He would not bend to the weight pressing down on him. He didn't waste time with denial. The walls were real. The bars were cold. And the deal was long gone. He had taken the risk. Played the game. Crossed the line.

Now he was here.

Brooklyn jail was about pressure. The kind that made men crack. The kind that came in the form of stale air, dead eyes, and a clock that never moved. Guards didn't need to throw punches; they just had to wait. The system did the rest.

But Sandman wasn't new to pressure. He'd built empires on it. The difference now was that there was no trade to hedge, no number to fix. Just time. Today, Sandman's out of prison and living in a halfway house somewhere in Northern California. They took a few million. Called it justice. But let's be honest, he might still be sitting on more. Russia, maybe. Or somewhere colder.

Either way, he's breathing. And that's enough—for now.

Chapter 9: Close Calls and Crazy Nights

Back in the early days of the internet, before regulations cracked down and everyone got wise, there was a guy who had the email game on lock. He wasn't just some script kid running phishing scams—he was *the* guy. The king of spam. If you ever got an email about fake Rolexes, offshore bank accounts, or a Nigerian prince, chances were it came from his operation. And he made millions doing it.

I met him years ago when I was with Sandman. We were in Miami, and Sandman took me to this guy's house—if you could even call it a house. It was a mansion, the kind you see in rap videos, with white columns out front, a massive infinity pool overlooking the water, and a garage that looked like a luxury car showroom. Ferraris, Lambos—you name it. But his favorite? A pure-white Rolls-Royce Phantom with custom plates that basically screamed, *I made it.*

The first thing I noticed about him, besides the insane setup, was his hand. Or rather, what was missing from it. His right hand had no thumb and no index finger. Just a pinky, ring, and middle finger, like a damn claw. I didn't say anything at first, but I definitely noticed. It was the kind of thing you don't just ignore.

Later that night, after a few drinks, I asked Sandman, "What's the deal with his hand?"

Sandman just smirked and leaned in. "Word is, he screwed over some wise guys. They caught up with him, took his trigger finger and thumb so he could never shoot a gun again. Let him keep the rest so he could count money."

Jesus.

I looked over at him—this guy living the high life, drinking expensive champagne, laughing with models draped over him—like nothing had ever happened. But I could tell. It *had* happened. And he knew it.

Still, he kept pushing his luck. Spamming wasn't enough for him anymore. He started playing the stock market—low-float, high-volatility penny stocks before they were the mainstream hustle they are now. He figured out a system, probably had insiders feeding him tips, and he printed money. He ran the kind of pump-and-dump scams that would eventually put guys like him behind bars, but back then? The SEC hadn't caught up yet. He seemed untouchable.

And he lived like it.

He was taking out supermodels, popping bottles at the Versace Mansion, and rolling through South Beach like he owned it. If you were in Miami back then, you either knew him or wanted to. He was a character straight out of a movie—except in real life, guys like him don't get happy endings.

Last I heard, he vanished. Some say he cashed out, moved overseas, and is still living large. Others claim the same guys who took his fingers eventually came back to finish the job.

Either way, the legend of the Rolls-Royce Spammer? That's never going away.

***

It was the early 2000s, and I was rolling with Sandman and The Canuck, the hockey player. Through some connection, we got an invite down to Costa Rica to meet with a firm. Sounded like a good excuse for a trip, so we booked our flights and headed south.

As soon as we landed, we found ourselves at this wild hotel-casino—one of those places you can tell has seen some serious shit. The place was packed with hookers, just out in the open, no pretense. It was like Vegas without the rules. We were having drinks, taking it all in, when these guys finally showed up to get us. They pulled up in an old Jeep, and the second we got in, we all had the same thought: *Are we about to get murdered?*

They drove us out of the city and into some ghetto, winding through sketchy streets and climbing higher into the hills. We weren't sure if we were being kidnapped or just on our way to some remote mansion, but there wasn't much we could do at that point. Finally, after what felt like an eternity, we pulled up to this massive gated compound.

The place was called the White House, and it looked exactly like a mini version of the real deal. Guards stood at the entrance with machine guns, no joke. As we pulled in, we looked at each other like, *What the hell did we just get ourselves into?*

Inside, the place was unreal. Each room was named after a U.S. president—Reagan, Kennedy, Nixon, you name it. Hookers strolled around like part of the décor, and massive lobster tanks lined the walls. The steak and lobster they served were some of the best I'd ever had. If you wanted company for the night, no one was stopping you. It was a free-for-all.

The next day, we finally met the guys who had invited us down. Their office had armed guards at the front door—not exactly a welcoming vibe. We took the elevator up, and the moment we stepped inside, I could feel it. These guys were shady. Something about the whole setup screamed trouble.

After sitting through the meeting, I pulled Sandman and The Canuck aside and told them straight up: I wouldn't put a single dollar with these guys. I didn't know what their real business was, but it wasn't anything I wanted to be part of. We wrapped things up, flew home, and didn't give it much more thought.

Then, about a month later, I turned on the news and there he was, the owner of the firm. Busted in New York, caught on his private jet with a kilo of cocaine and a laundry list of federal charges. It was all over the headlines.

Wild trip. But in the end, just another close call.

Chapter 10: The Queen of Miami

Miami in the early 2000s was like the Wild West—only with Lamborghinis, offshore accounts, and illegal activities that most people can't wrap their heads around. It wasn't just a city; it was an empire built on excess. And no one embodied that more than her.

They called her the Queen of Miami. On paper, she was a powerhouse in the stock promotion game—smart, connected, and rich beyond belief. But the real fortune wasn't coming from her market plays. It was coming through the harbor.

Her operation was bold. She paid longshoremen not in cash, but in stock from her companies. In exchange, those longshoremen made sure her 'shipments' slipped into Miami Harbor without so much as a raised eyebrow.

The first time I met her, I was with Sandman. She invited us to her mansion, a sprawling estate right on the water in one of Miami's most exclusive neighborhoods. It didn't just scream wealth—it threatened you with it. Marble floors. An infinity pool overlooking the bay. A yacht out back. Even a rock-star-style RV parked in the driveway. Security cameras covered every angle.

Everything about it felt staged. Like a set. I had this nagging feeling the whole time, like I was being watched. Not just by security—*really* watched. Recorded. The way she moved, the way she spoke... something was off. It wasn't paranoia; I knew when a room had ears.

But in Miami, you didn't ask too many questions. You just smiled, shook hands, and handled business. I wasn't drinking at that point in my life. My thing back then was rolling into towns, grabbing an apple from the hotel, and using it to smoke. That night, she took a hit from my apple pipe and got *blasted*. Next thing I know, she's running around her mansion, stoned out of her mind. Her husband was the one behind *Red Shoe Diaries*, that soft-core series from the late '80s and '90s.

Anyhow, a few months later, it all came crashing down. She and her husband were everywhere—front page of the news, splashed across every financial crime report in the country. Turns out, she'd been cutting deals with longshoremen at the port, paying them not in cash, which could be traced, but in stock from her companies. Clean on paper, untouchable in theory.

In exchange, her shipments, sometimes a full ton of cocaine, slipped into Miami Harbor without so much as a raised eyebrow. The longshoremen were getting rich, and no one asked questions because, technically, she wasn't handing over a dime.

But greed always pushes too far. The feds had been watching, connecting the dots, and when they finally moved in, they took down everyone—her, her husband, half the damn port. It was a spectacle.

I sat back and watched the headlines roll in, shaking my head. I knew it. That feeling I had in her mansion? That wasn't paranoia. That was my gut telling me something was coming.

And in Miami, when the fall happens, it isn't quiet. It's a damn explosion.

Chapter 11: The Wild Side of Panama & Colombia

Panama was always a trip, but Colombia? That was a whole different level of insanity.

We stayed at the Trump Hotel in Panama whenever we were in town—always in the best suites, always living like kings. It was the kind of place where the drinks never stopped, and the service was so polished you almost felt guilty. Almost. But Panama was just the warm-up act. The real madness was in Colombia.

There was this bar called Habano's. In reality, this bar was a high-end whorehouse, known for having hookers, but it was disguised just enough to keep up appearances. Every month, like clockwork, we'd roll in, and the entire place would erupt. The girls would stand up, clapping like we were rock stars. It was like walking into your own surprise birthday party every single time. Hilarious. They treated us like kings, and we didn't do much to discourage it.

Colombia, though—that's where things got really crazy. We were working down there, handling business, but the office we were dealing with? It was straight out of a movie. Picture this: some guy walking around, casually carrying a silver platter full of cocaine. Not a few grams. Not a little baggie. A damn platter. Just floating around the office, like he was offering hors d'oeuvres. Everyone could take a bump whenever they wanted. No big deal. Just another day at the office.

At first, it was surreal, but after a while, nothing surprised me anymore. It was Colombia. You could be sitting in a high-rise office, making million-dollar deals, and five minutes later, be in the back of some armored SUV, racing through the streets with guys carrying machine guns.

The contrast between wealth and absolute lawlessness was staggering. The people we were dealing with weren't your average corporate types. These were guys who had seen and done things that would make Wall Street sharks look like choirboys. They operated in a world where money flowed as fast as blood, and you had to know exactly where you stood at all times. Respect was everything. A wrong word, a bad handshake, or even the perception of disrespect could cost you a lot more than just a deal.

And yet, somehow, we thrived in that chaos. It was a rush. The parties, the power plays, the sheer audacity of it all—it was like being in a high-stakes game with no rules, and we were winning. At least for now.

Every time we left, I'd think, *That was insane.* No way it gets crazier than this. And every time, I was wrong.

Chapter 12: The Greek

The Greek was a tough and cheap man. He had that old-school New York grit—the kind of guy who'd shake your hand with one while picking your pocket with the other. A hustler. A survivor.

When the 2008 market crashed, I was looking for any way to make money. I'd lost everything in the stock market, and I wasn't the type to sit around feeling sorry for myself. I was built, in shape, and—if I'm being honest—I didn't mind violence now and then. I was good at it.

That's probably why the Greek came to me.

He taught me how to run collections on people who owed him serious money. He had a stock promoter who'd burned him—ripped off a ton of people and skipped town with their money. He told me the guy was hiding in Vegas, and he needed someone to go collect. The deal was simple: find the guy, get the money, split it 50-50.

Sounded easy enough.

We rented a car and drove from L.A. to Vegas. The Greek chain-smoked the entire way—cheap cigarettes that smelled like burning rubber. It was disgusting. I had to keep the window cracked just to breathe, but every time I did, he'd complain about the wind messing up his hair. By the time we hit the Nevada state line, I was ready to puke.

The target was an Asian guy, flamboyant as hell, cruising around in a bright-colored Lamborghini, flashing money that wasn't his. Vegas is the perfect place for a guy like that to disappear—too many distractions, too many people who don't ask questions. We spent two days trying to track him down, hitting every connection we had in town. Nothing. He was good at hiding—probably knew someone would come looking for him.

We left Vegas empty-handed, but the Greek wasn't done with me.

A few weeks later, he called again. Another job. This time it was a guy in L.A. who owed him a few hundred grand. The Greek wanted me to pay him a visit. I won't lie—I was scared shitless. I had no idea what to expect walking into that situation. But I needed the money, and fear has a way of sharpening your focus.

We pulled up to a guy's house in L.A.—he owed the Greek $400K. The deal was simple: get the money, split it 50/50. I needed cash, so I was in.

We knocked. His wife answered the door, and he appeared behind her. It was awkward as hell—kids were right there too. I kept it respectful and told him we needed a word. He sent his family to the store, and we had a man-to-man conversation.

No threats. No shouting. Just straight talk.

He agreed to pay. The job went smoother than I expected.

But here's where I learned the real lesson—the Greek was a slimy man. Out of that $400K, he tossed me five grand. That was it. He didn't honor our 50-50 deal. That was the thing with him: he always dangled the promise of big paydays, but when it came time to settle up, he suddenly forgot how to count.

That day I learned two things:

1. You can get results without violence.
2. Never trust the Greek again.

After that, he kept trying to drag me into his stock promotions, but I wasn't interested. I didn't trust him. He was a snake.

Last I heard, he was working for the feds. I wasn't surprised. Guys like him always find a way to save their own skin.

I never answered his calls again.

Chapter 13: Dirty Little Tacos in Tijuana

I'd always known that some of the shadiest people in the game weren't the ones in the headlines—they were the ones behind the scenes, pulling strings and signing contracts that made fortunes appear and disappear. Dirty Little Tacos was one of those guys. A Mexican attorney who didn't just navigate the legal system—he bent it to his will. He made things happen, whether they were above board or so deep in the gray areas of the law that you'd need a flashlight to find the truth.

Dirty Little Tacos was short—maybe five-five on a good day—but his ego was six-five. Always dressed to impress: custom suits, gold cufflinks, designer loafers, and a Rolex you could spot across the room. Smart? Absolutely. Smarter than he thought? Not a chance. You see, guys like him forget that when you play too many sides at once, eventually someone comes collecting. Word was, the authorities had been after him for years. He'd been keeping a low profile in Mexico, still doing his business, still making money and still living in style.

I crossed paths with him in Tijuana, of all places—inside a luxury gated apartment complex reserved for people with serious money. I was there with an acquaintance from Cabo, a man whose reputation alone was enough to make the toughest men second-guess their life choices. The second we stepped onto the terrace where Dirty Little Tacos was drinking his overpriced tequila, I saw the color drain from his face.

He recognized me right away, but it wasn't me he was worried about—it was the man standing next to me. My friend didn't say a word. He didn't need to. His reputation did the talking.

Dirty Little Tacos tried to keep it together, flashing that trademark cocky grin and leaning back in his chair, acting like he was still in control. Beside him sat a woman half his age, dressed to turn heads. She might have been one of many he had "wifed up" over the years. This guy had a thing for turning working girls into personal investments, setting them up in apartments, paying for plastic surgery, making them feel like queens—for as long as they were useful. When they weren't, they disappeared just as quickly as they had arrived.

But that night, the easy charm wasn't working. He knew that if the guy from Cabo was looking for him, it wasn't for pleasantries.

"Blanco! Qué pedo, amigo!" he called out, forcing a smile. "What brings you to TJ?"

I just smirked. "Just visiting. Didn't know you were still around."

He chuckled nervously. "I keep a low profile these days, you know how it is."

Oh, I knew the rumors. I knew the feds were breathing down his neck for orchestrating hundreds of millions in pump-and-dump schemes. He is now hiding in Mexico, protected by the cartel. He had his hands in everything. And now, he was running out of places to hide.

That day, my buddy pulled out a cigar, lit it slowly, and just stared at him. The silence stretched, and Dirty Little Tacos started shifting in his seat.

"Good to see you, hermano," I finally said, slapping him on the shoulder just hard enough to remind him we weren't on the same side.

We left him there, sitting on that terrace, trying to act like he wasn't about to piss himself.

As we walked out, my buddy finally spoke. "Ese güey? He's already dead. He just doesn't know it yet."

I glanced back at Dirty Little Tacos, still holding onto his drink like it was the last thing keeping him grounded. Yeah, he was balling, but the feds weren't his only problem.

I had a feeling the next time I heard about Dirty Little Tacos, it wouldn't be over drinks.

Chapter 14: New Year's Lockup at the Happiest Place on Earth

Disney World is supposed to be magical—the kind of place where kids' dreams come true, where families make memories, and where people wear matching Mickey-ear shirts like they've joined some kind of cult.

For me? It turned into a four-day jail stint, all because of a stripper's New Year's greeting, a pissed-off woman I was with, and some very unfortunate timing.

New Year's Eve had started out fine—or as fine as it can when you're with a woman who treats every interaction with another female like an act of war. She was stunning but the woman I was with had fire in her veins, and I'd already learned the hard way that her temper had no off switch.

The plan was simple: fireworks, overpriced champagne, and a night in one of those fancy Disney resort rooms. Instead, I ended up in an orange jumpsuit, freezing my ass off in a Florida jail cell.

It all started with a message.

A stripper, my ex-girlfriend, sent me a New Year's picture. For that woman, it was a declaration of war.

The picture was… festive. "Happy New Year!" written across her chest in red lipstick. Nothing else.

I barely had time to process it before she saw it over my shoulder. One second, she was sipping champagne like a lady; the next, she was hurling glasses across the room like a Major League pitcher. Crystal shattered everywhere, the bottle went flying, and suddenly the suite looked like a crime scene.

I had locked the girl I was with on the balcony in her fur coat while she was screaming. I stepped on a champagne glass. Blood smeared across the floor. She was still screaming, the room was trashed, and then—bam, bam, bam—someone knocked at the door.

Disney security.

They walked in to find a wrecked room, a bleeding guy (me), and a wild-eyed Latina mid-meltdown. Their walkie-talkies crackled, more security showed up, then the cops. Before I knew it, I was in handcuffs, trying to explain that I wasn't the crazy one in this situation. Didn't matter. It was New Year's Eve, which meant I was stuck in the system until Tuesday.

***

Florida jail in January is freezing. Not Minnesota cold, but when you're wearing a thin jumpsuit and lying on a slab, it feels like the damn Arctic. No blanket. No warmth. Just misery.

And all because of a badly timed text from a stripper.

For four days, I sat in that cell, replaying how a "magical" night at Disney had turned into a nightmare. When I finally got out, I was pissed. The woman I was with had bailed while I rotted in jail. Classic. However, she watched Ethan (my son) while I was in jail for four days.

I walked out hungry, tired, and still picking glass out of my foot. I didn't even bother going back to the hotel—I just caught a flight home.

Disney had officially lost its magic for me.

We flew back to California, and it was very awkward.

Chapter 15: The Businessman Revelation & How I Got into Working on Wall Street

In my early twenties, I was juggling a lot—working at the gym during the day, bouncing at a club at night, and promoting parties in San Diego. I was young, hungry, and always looking for the next hustle. If there was money to be made, I wanted in.

One night, while working the door at the club, a group of older women—real pretty, drunk, and feeling bold—caught my eye. They were laughing and swaying to the music. As I stood there, arms crossed, watching the entrance, one of them turned to me, her eyes glassy but locked onto mine.

"You don't belong here," she slurred.

I smirked. "Oh yeah? Where do I belong then?"

"You should be a businessman," she said, her friends nodding in agreement.

I laughed it off at first, but the idea stuck with me. Maybe it was because I already knew it deep down. I loved deals. I loved negotiations—the back-and-forth, the adrenaline of making things happen. Whether it was setting up a packed club night or pulling off a big event, it was all the same game: strategy, risk, and reward.

That night, after the club closed, I couldn't shake what they had said. The next morning, I grabbed a local paper and started flipping through the classifieds. Buried between ads for used cars and apartment rentals, I found it:

"LEARN WALL STREET. HIGH COMMISSION. NO EXPERIENCE NECESSARY."

That was all I needed to see. I didn't own a suit, let alone a proper dress shirt or tie, so I borrowed them from a buddy. I threw together a résumé full of creative "experience"— stretching the truth, adding whatever I thought sounded good. The goal was simple: get in the door.

The address on the ad led me to a high-rise in La Jolla, a fancy office building that looked completely out of place for a guy like me. When I walked in, I was met by two brothers who owned the firm—complete opposites in every way. One looked like he had been dipped in a can of spray tan, head-to-toe Gucci, dripping in gold jewelry, grinning like he was auditioning for a movie about himself. The other was the complete opposite—meek, pale, dressed in a conservative gray suit, looking like he'd never stepped outside without checking the stock market first.

The conservative brother was the one interviewing me. He asked the usual questions—"What makes you think you can sell?" "Why do you want to be in this business?"—but I didn't overthink it. I just hustled him like I had hustled my way into every other opportunity in my life. I told him exactly what he wanted to hear, with the confidence of a guy who had already won.

They hired me on the spot. I started that Monday.

The office was pure boiler-room energy—no computers, just stacks of paper with leads scribbled on them. An old-school recovering alcoholic, a guy who had been through the wringer, took me under his wing. He handed me my first sheet of leads, leaned in, and told me, "This is the game, kid."

And I got good—really good. The phone became my weapon. I learned how to build trust, create urgency, and close deals before the guy on the other end even knew what hit him.

Money was flowing—or at least it should have been. That's when I started noticing something off. These guys weren't paying me. They'd throw me $500 here and there, just enough to keep me grinding, but when I did the math, they owed me at least ten grand—which, at the time, might as well have been a million dollars to me.

Long story short, after a couple of years, I realized what was really happening. These guys weren't just skimming off me— they were taking advantage of clients. Fake trades, inflated commissions, straight-up fraud. I had seen some shady things in my life, but this was next-level.

I wasn't going to be a part of it. So, I packed my bags and walked into another firm. If I was going to play the game, I was going to do it my way—and on my terms.

Chapter 16: The Hustle— Making Millions & Bending the Rules

Wall Street wasn't just about numbers—it was about psychology. The flickering red and green of the stock ticker didn't tell the real story; the emotions behind the trades did. Markets weren't driven by spreadsheets or earnings reports. They were driven by fear and confidence, and I had spent years learning to read both like a seasoned street hustler sizing up a mark.

It was a high-stakes casino where the house always won, but unlike a Vegas dealer, I wasn't just playing the odds—I was influencing them. The difference between a windfall and a wipeout wasn't intelligence or strategy. It was the ability to anticipate the herd's next move before they even knew it themselves. Would they panic? Would they hold? Would they chase? I didn't need to ask—I already knew.

I saw them daily: the nervous investors hugging their screens as lifelines, peering hopefully for any hint of calm, fingers poised over the sell key, anticipating the moment they would tip. The confident ones marched through trading rooms thinking they had the solution, only to be brought low when the market shifted against them. And then there were the desperate ones—the ones who had borrowed too much, bet too big, and now had everything to lose. Their fear was the easiest to exploit.

I made my money not by beating the market but by beating the people in it. I knew when to stoke fear and when to sell confidence. A well-placed rumor here, a shift in momentum there—it didn't take much to push the weak hands into panic-selling or to convince the greedy ones they were missing out. The market wasn't rational, no matter how much the economists wanted to believe it was. It was emotional. And emotions could be manipulated.

I had seen it happen too many times to count. A whisper of bad news, a leaked report, a strategic sell-off at just the right moment—it didn't matter if the fundamentals were sound. The perception was reality. A company could be thriving, but if people believed it was in trouble, the stock would plummet. And if enough of the right people believed in a rally, even the weakest stock could soar.

The winners weren't always the brightest or the most seasoned. They were the ones who understood how to manage the narrative, how to make fear an opportunity, and how to remain ahead of the game. Because, at the end of the day, the game wasn't about the market. It was about the players. And I had learned how to play them all.

Most traders played by the rules. They read charts, tracked trends, trusted technical analysis, and kept their trades neat. They revered the altar of moving averages, Fibonacci retracements, and relative strength indicators, thinking that numbers could foretell the future.

But the real money? It wasn't in following the rules—it was in knowing how to bend them without breaking them.

There were a hundred ways to make a stock move, and I knew them all. The market was supposed to be efficient, with a perfect pricing mechanism reflecting all available information. That was the biggest lie ever sold to retail traders. Information wasn't equal—some people had it first, some people controlled how it spread, and others, like me, knew how to make it work in their favor.

I had a front-row seat to the games guys played on the Street. I watched as some of them ran the same hustle over and over - find a company no one was watching, something thinly traded, undervalued, just sitting there like bait. No blue-chip stocks, nothing the big institutions were into. The quieter the ticker, the easier it was to move.

I'd see it all happen - the whispers start, the coordinated buying to drive the price up, the fake buzz. Classic pump-and-dump. Guys made a quick buck, looked like geniuses for a minute. But I also saw how it ended. Same script every time. The feds knocking, the charges piling up. I never touched that mess myself. Just watched it burn guys who thought they were untouchable.

It began with rumors. A discreet chat in an upscale restaurant, loud enough for the proper ears to hear. A hint is given to a hungry reporter seeking their next major story. An anonymous post in a financial forum, buried among the noise but positioned perfectly for those who knew how to read between the lines.

Then came the brokers—the lifeblood of the machine. I hit the right ones with 'friendly tips.' Some would take the bait because they thought they were ahead of the game. Others would push it further, hyping up their clients and creating momentum out of thin air. And just like that, the stock would move.

But it wasn't enough for it to rise—it had to soar. That's where the real work happened. I got analysts talking, nudging them toward the right conclusions without ever saying too much. I'd ensure the news cycle picked up steam, feeding carefully curated information to financial media outlets and ensuring the right talking heads were echoing the narrative I wanted.

Retail traders would see the action and pile in, thinking they'd discovered the next big thing. They'd believe it was their instincts, their research, their skill that led them to the trade. That was the beauty of it. By the time they bought in, I was already positioned to exit. Because, in the end, it wasn't about luck or even intelligence. It was about control. And those who controlled the story controlled the market.

The market was a herd mentality. It didn't matter how sophisticated investors pretended to be, how many degrees or algorithms they had—at the core, they were just followers. The second those first few players saw movement, they jumped in like lemmings, convinced they were ahead of the game. And once the frenzy started, it became a self-fulfilling prophecy.

A rumor, a shift in momentum, a strategic trade—none of these was necessary. The perception was all that was required. Investors swarmed in, stampeding in pursuit of the surge, believing they had discovered some hidden secret before everyone else was aware of it.

Everybody at the top was in on this game. Hedge funds, private equity shops, and corporate insiders all had their methods of manipulating the market to their advantage. They kept the system in place to benefit themselves, not the marks still holding onto the idea of fair play. The difference between them and me? I wasn't afraid to go all in.

One of my biggest scores came on a pharmaceutical stock that was about to pop. The company was set to release clinical trial results for a new cancer drug. Most of the market had no clue what was coming. But I did. A whisper from someone inside. A hint buried in an offhand remark at a private event. I connected the dots, and the picture was clear: it was good news. Groundbreaking results. Life-changing medication. A stock that would double, maybe even triple, overnight.

I went in heavy. Seven figures. No hedging, no options, just pure conviction. The kind of trade that could make me untouchable or bury me if it went south. The seconds leading up to the news release stretched out like an eternity. Every heartbeat was a countdown.

Then, the announcement hit the wire.

Boom.

The stock exploded.

In a matter of minutes, we had doubled my investment. As we watched, my screen filled with green, my numbers climbing, my equity skyrocketing. The market was scrambling to catch up. Analysts were racing to update their forecasts. Talking heads were calling it a "breakthrough moment." Retail traders, the last ones to the party, were still trying to get a piece of the action.

By lunch, our team had made a few million dollars. More money in hours than most people made in a lifetime.

That was the high. That was the rush. That was the reason I never wanted to stop. It wasn't just about the money—it was the control, the power of seeing the game unfold exactly as I had planned. Because when you knew how to play the market, you didn't just make money. You made reality.

High stakes meant high risks. And if you weren't careful, you weren't just losing money—you were making enemies. At first, it was the usual calls. Hedge fund guys, private investors, sharks who smelled blood in the water. Some wanted in on my next play, and others just called to congratulate me, trying to get close and figure out how I was always a step ahead. That was normal. That was expected. But then the calls started coming from people who didn't wear suits. The kind of people who used to solve problems with guns instead of lawyers. That's when I realized I wasn't just playing a financial game anymore. I was playing a survival game.

One day, I got a call from a guy I barely knew—a connected guy, the kind who doesn't leave voicemails. The guy's voice was calm, but there was an edge to it, like a knife pressed just lightly against my skin.

"I got a problem," he said. "And you're gonna fix it."

It turns out that a stock I had played a little too aggressively had left some people on the wrong side of the trade. Not the SEC. Not the regulators. Real people. People who didn't take losses lightly. People who didn't believe in second chances.

I had always thought of myself as untouchable, a guy who could outthink the system and walk away clean. But this was different. Wall Street wasn't just about money anymore. It was about power. And power attracts predators.

We met at a quiet steakhouse in Midtown. Not some dark alley. Not a basement poker room. A high-end restaurant with white tablecloths, soft candlelight, and the quiet hum of wealth in the air. Waiters poured wine, a jazz band played in the background, and no one had any idea that at one of those polished mahogany tables, a man was deciding whether or not I would keep breathing. That's how I knew he was the real deal. He didn't need to hide.

He sat across from me, slicing into his filet like he had all the time in the world. When he finally looked up, his expression didn't change.

"You made me lose a lot of money," he said, dabbing his mouth with a linen napkin.

I swallowed hard and kept my face neutral. "That's how the market works," I said.

The man smirked, a knowing, almost amused look.

"Nah, kid. That's how your game works. And I don't lose."

Then he leaned in, lowering his voice just enough to make sure I caught every word.

"So now, you owe me."

I didn't argue. What was I going to say? No?

The man laid it out in plain terms. There was no negotiation. No way out. I was going to make it right. And in return? I would keep breathing.

I nodded. That was all he needed.

At first, it seemed simple. He wanted me to push a stock—hard. Not some small-time penny stock, but a real company. Something with weight behind it. His people had a position, and they needed it to move—fast.

My job? Put together an investor package and help tell the story to the whole of Wall Street. Get the right players talking. Let the right funds know. Build momentum.

I knew how to do that — and I did. I pulled every string I had. Got analysts talking. Paid for 'independent' research reports. The buying pressure built. Retail traders piled in, thinking they'd found the next big thing. Within a week, the stock had doubled. Tens of millions were made.

I thought that was it. Debt paid. I was wrong. A few days later, another call.

"You did good," the man said. "Real good."

I nodded, already thinking about how I'd walk away clean. But then he just chuckled, low and knowing.

"We're gonna do this again."

And that's when it hit me. This wasn't a one-time job. This wasn't a favor I could repay and move on. I had stepped over a line, and there was no stepping back. I wasn't just a trader anymore. I was in a different game now—a game with no exit.

The Breaking Point

Chapter 17: The Breaking Point – The Britney Spears Breakdown

By the time I realized I was in too deep, it was already too late. I wasn't just making money anymore—I was making moves for people who didn't take "no" for an answer. The market had been a game to me. A means of demonstrating my intelligence, my ability to read people, trends, and placing the right bets at the right moments. I had been seeking the rush of the deal, the sense of beating everyone else and getting away with it. I actually had a natural talent at this—money had been my easiest thing on the planet, and the approval had felt so good. But it was no longer the game. It wasn't more money, more profit. My trades didn't just involve profit anymore; they involved the power plays.

I had sold out to men who didn't care about the rules. They didn't care about morality, legality, or ethics. They fixed problems with bullets rather than lawsuits. This was a world I had entered willingly. And now, it was a world that was consuming me. The pressure of it weighed down on my chest, each second drawing me deeper into a reality I wasn't ready for.

I didn't even know I had crossed the line between two worlds. It was so slow, so fluid. One wrong choice led to another, and before long, I was entrenched in a criminal web of crime, corruption, and shadowy deals I could hardly even imagine.

I thought I was untouchable at first. The cash came in quicker than I could tally. It wasn't only the riches—it was the authority. The feeling that I could do whatever, be whoever. That I could enter any room and be noticed. The perception that I was invincible, beyond the law. I was rising higher and higher, but the higher I rose, the more tenuous the ascent was.

The more I produced, the deeper in I went. The more I produced, the more my world was unsafe. The bets increased in danger, the ones I made riskier, the people I sold to more erratic, and the stakes? Financial first, but personal soon afterward.

Every transaction brought me deeper into a universe where right and wrong didn't exist. There was no wrong or right anymore—there was only leverage and loyalty. And loyalty? Loyalty wasn't trust. Loyalty wasn't being there for each other no matter what. Loyalty was fear. Fear of the repercussions. Fear of what would happen if you didn't play by the rules.

The men I worked with—those in charge—did not care about who I was or what I had done. They cared about what I could provide for them, what I could do for them. And if I couldn't provide, there was always someone else who could.

I wasn't sleeping. I wasn't eating. The pressure was crushing. I could sense it in every molecule of my body. It never eased. There was always something to accomplish, someone to placate, a sale to make. I was a machine, one that ran on adrenaline and terror. I was doing more blow than Tony Montana—taking every line as just another means to anesthetize the mounting anxiety within me, another means to keep the panic at arm's length.

My phone never stopped ringing. It was relentless—deals, threats, pressure. Everybody wanted something from me, and I had to keep fueling the beast. Every call was like a countdown, counting down to the inevitable. The market was a beast that had to be fed, and I was the one holding the leash.

Each transaction was like tiptoeing across a sharks' den. Each choice was the last I might ever make. Make the wrong move, and I wouldn't merely lose everything—I'd die. The stakes continued to escalate, and the risks became more lethal.

And then the paranoia began. Was I being followed? Were my phones bugged? Was the FBI on my case? It began as a little nagging sensation in the back of my head. A whisper that made me look over my shoulder, a look at the phone that made me shiver. It was simple to brush off initially. The mind tricks you, right? But then it began to escalate. Every strange car on the road seemed like a sign. Every look from a stranger made my heart skip a beat.

I wasn't the only one doing this. I knew that. The men I worked for—they didn't trust anyone, not even me. I was a piece to be used, and the one thing they appreciated was loyalty. But loyalty here wasn't a matter of trust. It wasn't a matter of friendship or alliances. It was a matter of fear. Fear of what would occur if I didn't comply.

I had created an empire, but I was beginning to realize that I wasn't the one holding the reins. I had created a cage for myself. And every up was shorter, every down deeper. I couldn't shake the feeling that the walls were closing in.

That's when I knew I had to do something drastic.

***

My wife had broken down at Costco. My kids were babies at the time—our car had overheated. I had taken two Xanax and two Theraflu because I was getting sick and had a meeting that night. By the time I swapped cars with my wife, the tow truck was already two hours late. I was so fucked up I could barely stand, leaning against the bumper as we waited.

I got to the Beamer dealership, and my buddy, who was the manager, tossed me the keys of a brand-new X5. He looked at me and said, "Man, you look high as fuck." I told him, "Two Xanax, two Theraflu, and I've got a meeting I'm already late for."

I made it to the meeting and had a glass of wine—terrible idea. By the time I left, I was really out of it. I drove that rental X5 like I had stolen it, blasting music down my hill. Took a turn too fast, hit the curb, and launched the brand-new X5 through my neighbor's roof.

I was so fucked up I tried to reverse out of the roof. Couldn't even open the driver's side door. So I wiped the steering wheel down with my T-shirt, grabbed my cell phones, and climbed out the back, scratching my ass on a nail jumping down.

Ran home. My wife asked where the Beamer was. I told her, "We'll talk about it in the morning. Don't worry."

My house was on a hill—I could see everything. Cops were swarming the scene, and even a helicopter was overhead. The lot up the street was empty, so I casually walked up there to check things out, trying to play it cool. Ten cops had their guns on me. Helicopter spotlight on my face.

They yelled, "Freeze!"

I threw my hands up and started walking toward them, being super polite. "Hey guys, easy now."

One cop goes, "Damn, you've got a nice house."

"Thanks, man," I said.

They asked if I knew what happened down the street. I played dumb.

Later at the station, they said, "You wanna tell us what happened?" I said, "I want my lawyer."

My lawyer, Marc Applbaum, was my best friend. Back in San Diego, he got me out of court. All I had to pay was a $500 deductible to fix the house and the car. Best $500 I had ever spent.

***

I was on a first-class flight the night before the BMW crash when a guy told me he'd bought a lot overlooking the ocean for just 25K. After the accident, the only thing on my mind was Nicaragua—escaping to a new, faraway land.

On my first night there, I met this guy who had butlers constantly bringing him drinks. He was Nicaraguan but spoke perfect English. He looked at me and said, "Ben, you're lucky you met me. You're coming to a party with me tomorrow night."

The next evening, I get a call on WhatsApp. I head down to the hotel lobby and see two military helix trucks, blue and red lights flashing, armored vehicles everywhere. I'm thinking, *What the hell did I just get myself into? Is this the mafia?* My mind was racing.

We rolled up to this massive mansion with security everywhere. I'm not gonna lie, I was shitting myself. The guy I'd met the night before led me inside and introduced me to a man in full military fatigues. Turned out, he was the general of the Nicaraguan army.

He shook my hand—firm, serious—and said, "Welcome to Nicaragua. Whatever you need, we have for you." The General introduced me at his party to his mother. I never thought I would find myself partying with the General of the Nicaraguan army. It was a massive party. Live band, packed crowd. The General's mother came to get me. I was the only white boy there—no Spanish, no clue. She taught me to dance Muamba in the middle of the party.

The General then introduced me to a blonde Colombian woman... who, as it turned out, was a madame.

After being there for just three days, Nicaragua was already turning into something out of a fever dream. That's when I met a madame—yeah, like, an actual madame—with a whole crew of working girls. And let me tell you, the hookers were not cute. I mean we're talking bottom-of-the-barrel. But the madame? She was something else. Colombian. Big fake chest, platinum blonde hair, and this over-the-top Latin Barbie vibe. She had that kind of confidence that made you forget, for a second, how absolutely insane the whole situation was.

We started hanging out. Drinks, wild stories, her trying to show me "her world." It was fun in that chaotic way. "I shouldn't be here, but I am" kind of way. We were just friends. But after three days, she rolls up, pulls up her skirt, and shows me my name tattooed on her leg while high. I stared at it, totally stunned. That's when it hit me: holy f***, this just got real, like, way too real.

I got drunk and was spiraling. I stayed in Nicaragua for six months. I didn't live in a penthouse. I had a mansion in the suburbs. Saw hookers, anything to hide from the truth. I was running away from being a man, a father, a husband.

But sooner or later, it all catches up with you.

I woke up one morning, my head throbbing, my body battered and broken. For the first time in a long time, I saw the truth. The truth stared back at me in the mirror. I wasn't going to survive. I was either going to die or I was going to change.

It was the beginning of the end. The jungle did not fix me. The money did not fix me. I lost everything in order to realize what was important and mattered.

And that's exactly what was about to happen.

Chapter 18: Losing It All – The Fall from the Top

Coming back from the jungle did not mean I was safe. It only meant I was back in the game—whether I wanted to be or not. It was odd, actually. The jungle had been an escape, a refuge, a means to put distance between myself and what I had wrought. But even in the oppressive, hot air of the jungle, with its unnatural quietness and limitless green, the past had pursued. I wasn't unscathed. I wasn't untethered. I had hoped that if I distanced myself from the high-stakes game of money, it would give me the peace for which I had so desperately yearned. But peace, it now seemed, was a luxury too expensive for me to purchase anymore.

The fact is, I didn't want to return. But there I was, back in the game, whether I wanted it or not. The streets were not the same. The rush of Wall Street, the adrenaline that had once brought me to life, was now muffled, a dull thrum at the back of my head. I attempted to cling to the remnants of what I used to be. But it was slipping through my fingers. I was slipping.

I was back—but different this time. My trades weren't as quick as they had once been. My instincts, once impeccable, now seemed awry, as if I was attempting to find my way in a world that no longer held meaning. It was like swimming against a tide I couldn't manage. I had been so sure before. So self-assured. But now, I just couldn't seem to stop thinking that I was in too deep, and the deeper I went, the more I realized just how far gone I was.

I wasn't just slippin' in my skills—something was shifting inside me. I could sense it, deep down, a nagging sense of unease that wouldn't abate. My hold on reality, on the game itself, was slipping. And it wasn't only my play that was failing—it was the very basis of my existence. My deals, once so seamless, now seemed rickety foundations, buckling under the pressure of doubt. The tension once fuel for me now felt strangling, as a vice that sat around my chest.

But the worst of it wasn't the market pressure. It wasn't the loss or the fear of failure. No. The worst of it was the dawning awareness that the world I had become a part of, the world I had contributed to, was turning against me. I could sense it in the atmosphere—eyes upon me, constantly. A persistent, unseen presence. They were watching me. They were waiting. It wasn't paranoia any longer; it was true. A truth I couldn't deny.

The day my wife moved in, she didn't know what she was walking into. The chaos that I had created. I wanted to protect her from all of it, from seeing the person that I had become. But the thing is, when you have a chaotic life, you can't hide it forever. The cracks had started to appear, and despite how much I tried to keep up the act, the walls were collapsing.

When she moved in, I attempted to keep things somewhat normal. I drove the Aston Martin; I wore the suits tailored especially for me; I lived the high life in the mansion I'd purchased with my blood, sweat, and tears—or my deception, my fabrications, and my willingness to do whatever it took to push people aside in order to climb on top. I was living the dream still on the surface but falling apart inside.

What I didn't realize was that I was being watched. Phones tapped. Eyes on wherever I went. The men I had worked with, the men who had assisted in building my empire, were now asking for favors I couldn't provide. The favors weren't about money anymore. They were about power. They were about control. I had been used as a pawn in a game I was no longer familiar with, and no rules applied to this game. No backup plan. Only a perpetual game of high-stakes poker where one miscalculation results in losing everything.

The worst of it? I couldn't even tell my wife. I couldn't expose her to the reality. It was too risky. I wasn't shielding her from the turmoil; I was protecting her from knowing what I had become, what mess I had made. The reality that I couldn't escape.

But no matter how hard I tried to keep up appearances, the walls were closing in. The paranoia that had a faint whisper before was now an inescapable presence. Every time I caught a glimpse in the rearview mirror, I saw a car following me. Every time I left the house, I could sense eyes upon me, observing every move I made. It wasn't in my head—it was real.

It wasn't the police alone. It wasn't the individuals to whom I was in debt. There were others. The individuals who were desperate to make their mark in the world that I had built. The ones who had been waiting for me, watching me in the shadows, anticipating me to fall. They were there all the time, lurking, ready to take me down.

So one day, I went to the police station to get fingerprinted for the ridiculous old arrest at the Disneyland Hotel years ago— something I needed to get off my record so I could become an American citizen. I knew I was going to marry my wife, so I wanted everything cleared.

That's how I ended up getting pulled over, because that same day, the new Bluetooth law went into effect. I had my Bluetooth in, but first a bike cop stopped me, then undercover cars and cops came from every direction.

Earlier that day, I had been walking my dog with my wife, talking to my old high school friend and sales guy, Jay, about closing a deal. I joked, "We'll get them addicted, our crack and heroin," and my phone had been acting weird. Little did I know, one of my neighbors, who used to be in law enforcement, had tipped off Carlsbad police, claiming I was dealing drugs.

Why? Because there were always girls coming in and out of my house. In reality, they were my employees.

When they swarmed my vehicle, I didn't know what to do. There was no peace, no restraint. They zapped my mind, but my body was paralyzed. They dragged me out of the vehicle, hands on my shoulders, shoving me to the ground. I heard them shouting orders, but I couldn't concentrate.

I had always taken pride in being in charge—in being the one who made the decisions. But in that instant, I was nothing. I was just another individual swept along in a system larger than myself, a system that didn't care who I was or what I had accomplished.

They handcuffed me and stuffed me into the back of an unmarked car. It was a blazing summer day—110 degrees. Sweat beading down my neck, sticking to the leather of the seat, I sat there cooking, unable to move, unable to speak.

While I roasted in the heat, they illegally searched my home for two hours. My wife—who had just moved in the day before—arrived to see me surrounded by undercover officers, locked in the back of a police car. She had no idea what was happening. Neither did I. My son (about 7 years old) was in the other room, and all our members were handcuffed in my room.

They thought I was a drug dealer.

The local cops had been tapping my phone, convinced I was moving product in the suburbs. They saw the limo, the Aston Martin, the Mercedes, the steady stream of assistants and hot nannies, the lavish parties. To them, it all added up. To them, I had to be dirty. But they were wrong. They realized they had the wrong person and that case went away.

What they didn't understand was that I was just a kid from nowhere, barely out of high school, who'd clawed his way to Wall Street and was making ridiculous money. I was living the suburban dream—fast cars, big house, beautiful women—and yes, it rubbed people the wrong way. The married guys were envious. The wives? Not exactly fans. But I didn't care. I was doing my thing.

What really triggered the raid was the phone call with Jay. I had been joking around about getting a client "addicted to our crack or heroin." I had meant our marketing services.

I knew the local cops had my phone tapped, and the feds were sitting on a five-inch-thick file with my name on it. To them, my ties to both Wall Street and the streets made me look dirty. But I wasn't. I was just a guy in the wrong place at the wrong time.

Obviously, they didn't find any crack or heroin. There never was any.

When the detective finally brought me back to the house, I was still handcuffed. I turned to the officer and said, "My neighbors already think I'm a drug dealer. Please, just... have some respect. Drive me back in an undercover car."

The detective obliged.

As we pulled up, the officer turned and asked, "So... where's the crack and heroin?"

And right there, something snapped in me. A line had been crossed. I didn't yell. I didn't lash out. I just stared. Cold. That was the moment I knew—my phone would clear me. That all I had left was the truth.

"I did nothing wrong," I said. "I'm a clean businessman. I never did anything wrong."

They knew they'd messed up and trapped an innocent, dumb young dude's phone and life, and I was clean after that day the police illegally searched my house. This was 2008, the day the market crashed. I was doing a job for these Middle Eastern dudes from L.A. that seemed sketchy. I did my job—wrote up the company, hired guys to promote the stock—but the market crashed, and these idiots thought I had f*** them over.

The next day, they sent goons to my house on the second day my wife had lived there. They even came to my gym. I was getting in my Aston Martin when they asked if my name was Ben. I said, "No, it's Doug Stevens," and immediately called my wife, telling her not to open the door. She told me a Black guy and another man had just come by seconds earlier.

I called the cops. They were cool. I told them what happened, and they said, "You gotta get a gun— you live so far out here, by the time we get there, you'll be dead." They also told me to keep a video camera in case the guys came back.

Sure enough, they did.

I had just gotten out of the shower when my wife, my girlfriend at the time, told me there were guys at the door. I grabbed the video camera, my 9mm Kimber pistol with a laser, and opened the door—gun in hand, scared, shaking, filming.

It wasn't until after we'd watched the video multiple times that we saw the Black dude slowly pulling out a gun. I had the drop on him, and they left.

I got extremely angry that they came to my house when I'd done nothing wrong to them—other than try to do the right thing. I was so pissed off I jumped in my Porsche Cayenne SUV, gun in my lap, looking for these idiots. I was so angry—thank God I didn't find them, or I'd probably still be in jail.

But it didn't matter anymore. The damage was done. They had everything. Wiretaps. Recordings. Transcripts. Talks I thought were nonsense—just friendly chatter with high-up friends—were now evidence.

Jokes turned into charges.

I had two options.

One to go deeper into the fire. I could fight back. I could hustle my way back to the top, find another angle, and play the game harder. But I knew the cost. I knew what it would take. I would have to sell my soul to survive in that world.

Or walk away—I could break away from everyone I had ever known, start anew, and build again from nothing. I could walk away from the lies, the manipulation, and the greed. It was the most difficult decision I had ever had to make, but inside myself, I knew that was the only path forward.

I didn't realize it at the time, but God had already decided for me. But now, the question was: What would I do with what was left? Would I return? Or would I make the choice to leave it all behind?

There was only one path to take. I would have to redeem myself, rebuild, and find peace in a world that I had once destroyed. But first, I would have to make the most dangerous choice of all.

Chapter 19: One Last Job – The Final Exit

After losing everything—the money, the lifestyle, the power—I should have walked away for good. But the streets don't let you leave that easy. I was broke. My old contacts weren't returning my calls. But one guy did. A voice from the past. A big player.

"I know you're in a bad spot," the man said. "I got something for you. One last job. Make this move, and you're set. Disappear. Clean slate."

I knew better. I should have said no. But when you're staring at nothing, one last score sounds like a miracle.

The job wasn't small. It was deadly. A Russian gangster—one I had a serious history with—was back in the game. Igor. The same one I had gone to war with over a stock deal gone bad. The same one who had FBI ties. The same one who had just been arrested for lying about the Bidens' Ukraine deal.

I always knew Igor was a rat. But now, my old contact wanted me to help finish the war.

I called my closest brother in the game. He was in. We had our own limo, which was something out of a mob movie.

But then something happened, something I hadn't expected. A voice inside me said something I hadn't heard in years. *Walk away*. For the first time, I listened. I told my partner, "We're out."

He thought I was crazy. Maybe I was. But deep down, I knew—this was my last chance. I made a call. Canceled the meeting. Disappeared. All I knew was, if I had gone through with that meeting, I wouldn't be here to tell this story.

That was it. The moment I knew I had to leave. I had been given one last out. And this time? I took it. I left the life behind. For real. No more Wall Street games. No more gangsters. No more running. I had lost everything. But I was still alive. And that meant I had a second chance.

But just when I thought I was out, another fire flared up.

We had done a deal with a company—but behind the company was the Russian Doll in LA. I had heard rumors of her in the business. Slim, mid-fifties, always decked out in Gucci or Louis tracksuits. Smoking those little thin cigarettes. Wise. Cold. Dangerous.

She didn't come herself. She sent her enforcer - Igor. We didn't know she was back in town when the deal went through. At least not until Igor came knocking. Igor wasn't just some errand boy—he was muscle. A real Russian mobster. The kind that doesn't waste words or make empty threats. Stories floated around - how he shot guys in the knees without flinching.

He walked into Sandman's office like he owned the place. Locked the girls in the conference room. Black leather jackets. Gloves. Like something out of a movie. He didn't say much. Just let them know there was a meeting set for the next night in LA.

At the time, I wasn't there. I'd been at a doctor's appointment, ignoring my phone. By the time I got back to the car, I had 59 missed calls from Sandman. That's never a good sign.

When I called Sandman back, his voice was sharp: "Grab your bag of guns and your vest. Meet me at the office."

No questions asked.

I packed a bag—bulletproof vests, guns, rubber gloves, and a bottle of alcohol. We got into our limo and rode out toward LA. And that's when we prepped. We weren't expecting trouble, but we weren't taking chances either. In the back of the limo, we put on gloves and went to work - wiping bullets, loading mags, cleaning everything. No fingerprints. No screwups. We weren't walking in unarmed or unready. The German driver was freaked out but didn't say a word.

LA was different at night. The air felt thick like it carried every bad decision they'd ever made. We pulled up to the meeting spot. Stepped out. Walked in.

This is where the script flipped. I came in like a nerd with a spreadsheet full of numbers. I laid it all out. Line by line. Every transaction. Every move. The Russian scanned it. Said nothing at first. Just poured the vodka. Shot after shot. Then they started cracking jokes, poking fun at Wall Street jargon. The mood lightened. The Russian warmed up and started calling us "my friends." Maybe he thought he meant it. Maybe he believed he was one of us now.

But he was working for the FBI and the Russians. We had a feeling something was off, but at that moment, we were just playing the game. And that night? We won.

Turns out, the Russian Doll in LA - the real power behind the scenes - was the one orchestrating the whole mess. She'd been hiding behind another name in the deal, throwing heat off herself. She was quiet, smart and untouchable. But she made contact.

She called me directly.

In a cold voice and serious tone, she told me she had heard about me. Said she respected the numbers, the way I handled the heat. She didn't mess around but she respected the game.

Then something unexpected happened. She liked me. Said I had something the others didn't. Guts. Brains. Precision. She started bringing me more business. Bigger jobs. Cleaner plays. She didn't want chaos - she wanted control. And I was a tool she could use to get it.

We came into that meeting armed with truth and steel. But walked out with something more valuable: leverage.

That was the real exit. Not just walking away, but walking away with power. With knowledge. With enough clarity to know who had been pulling the strings all along.

I had dodged the bullet - literally and figuratively. And this time, I didn't just survive.

I upgraded.

Chapter 20: When the Past Came Knocking

I had finally done it. I walked away not just from a job or a city but from a life that had been devouring me without me even realizing it. The chaos was behind me now, or so I thought. There were no more dizzying adrenaline rushes on the trading floor, no more crooked smiles from gangsters I once called business partners, no more phone calls in the middle of the night with cryptic threats disguised as casual conversation, and no more deals made in the shadows. My wife and I were finally in a good place.

For the first time in years, my veins were clean. There was only ocean air, my family, and a life no longer lived in survival mode. I felt like my life meant something now. I was no longer chasing power or outrunning death. Life felt stable - calm, even.

In 2014, our family landed in Cabo, ready to begin a new chapter in our lives. I was starting over, trying to leave behind the chaos that had defined so many years before. Just days earlier, I had shaved my head in what I half-jokingly called my "Britney Spears breakdown." We enrolled the kids in a small private school, hoping to give them some stability. I didn't know a single person in town. I had no connections or friends except for the barest hope that I could keep my head down, stay sober, and finally learn how to be a father instead of a fugitive running from my own mistakes.

I didn't know a soul in town. My wife, though, had a gift for walking into any room and leaving with five new friends. One day, she came home buzzing about a Venezuelan woman she had met at the school.

"You have to meet my husband, Carlos," she said. "He races off-road, just like you. You guys would hit it off."

I didn't think much of it at the time. I had enough history and wasn't exactly jumping to make new friends. But a few weeks later, I agreed to meet Carlos for drinks. What happened next would stick with me for the rest of my life.

The restaurant we met at wasn't even open to the public that night. They had unlocked the doors just for us, and that should've been my first clue that Carlos wasn't your average weekend off-roader.

We sat down at a private table, ordered drinks, and started talking. Like most of my conversations back then, it didn't take long for the wild stories of my life to start spilling out. I began talking about my Wall Street runs, the bikers, the mafia connections, and the car crash that almost made me a headline. I wasn't bragging. I was just laying out who I was, unfiltered.

The more I shared my stories, the more his posture relaxed. Carlos finally leaned in and dropped his guard.

"I don't just race," he said. "I'm a high-ranking member of the Sinaloa Cartel."

He didn't flinch or whisper. He said it like someone talking about their family business. Then he laid it all out, including his routes, logistics, operations, and connections I wouldn't dare repeat. He told me he and El Chapo basically grew up together—same neighborhood, just a few streets apart, both from poor Sinaloa families scraping by. They'd been homies since day one. I never judged my friends—whether they were hustlers or mobsters. Funny thing is, now that I own a Jeep company, most of my circle is law enforcement and military.

When he finished the conversation, he looked at me like a recruiter sizing up a top prospect.

"You ever want in," he said, "I could make that happen." He offered me a seat at a poker table so casually, like it was just another deal to shuffle through.

I laughed and shook my head. "Carlos, I like my head right where it's at."

He smirked, took a slow sip of his drink, and we both laughed. But beneath the surface, I knew he wasn't joking. There was a cold edge to his smile that told me he was serious.

Despite the job offer, Carlos and I actually became friends. Real friends. Not the kind who shake hands and trade favors, but the kind who could sit for hours talking about trucks, dirt, life, and loss.

He was the most OG guy I had ever met. There were bullet wounds on his body like most guys have tattoos. He had been shot three or four times, and he carried the scars without ceremony. But he wasn't reckless or loud or sloppy. He was calculated. He was disciplined, and he had that kind of presence that made people sit up a little straighter when he walked in. He didn't need to raise his voice to command respect. His presence did that for him.

Life in Cabo was good, and I felt at peace. The ocean helped. So did the distance from the chaos I had run from. But nothing good ever stays, especially not in my world.

Eventually, my wife made the decision to move back to San Diego with the kids. I stayed behind for a while, trying to convince myself that I could handle things alone. But I could feel the heat rising, like the kind of pressure you learn to recognize when you've lived close to danger for too long.

So I left.

I packed up and moved closer to Tijuana just to be near my family. I didn't expect it, but Carlos's family ended up there too. Our lives crossed again. We'd see each other now and then, share a drink, and catch up like two guys with nothing to prove. It felt... safe. Or at least stable.

Then El Chapo got arrested. This was *the* takedown that made international headlines. The one that led to his extradition to the United States. And with that, the balance of power shifted overnight. He wasn't just a drug trafficker; he was the figurehead of an entire empire. His arrest sent shockwaves through every level of the Sinaloa Cartel. Territories that had once operated like well-oiled machines suddenly turned chaotic.

Like every power structure in that world, when the top falls, the rest scramble for control. It wasn't only the men at the top who felt the impact. The ripple effect reached everyone involved, including Carlos. His routes, connections, and the network he had spent years building were suddenly under pressure. Everyone knew something was changing, but no one could predict what would come next.

That was when Carlos got the call to go to Mexico City. He said there was a meeting there. But it turned out to be the last time anyone ever saw him.

His wife did everything she could to bring him back. She paid the ransom, emptied their bank accounts, and sent anything of value. She even parted with his entire watch collection, hoping it would be enough. I can still remember the look on her face when she told me all of this; it was desperate and hollow, but still holding on to hope like it was the only thing keeping her upright.

But Carlos never came home.

He vanished without a word. There were no goodbyes, no explanations, and no answers. That was the last time I ever heard his name spoken aloud.

Sometimes, I think about that first night we met. The closed restaurant, the laughs, the way he offered me a job like it was nothing. I had said no, and that decision saved me from a world that ultimately swallowed him whole.

I think Carlos was the kind of man who understood the price of doing business in the world he operated in. Like too many others I've known, he became another ghost in my story - another name I'll never forget, even if the world eventually does.

***

When we first moved to Cabo, I thought walking away was enough to keep the past at bay, but the past does not leave. It lurks and waits. And just when you start to breathe easier, when your guard slips for a second, it finds you. Sometimes, all it takes is a knock at the door... or the ring of a doorbell.

It was just after sunset in Cabo San Lucas. The sky was bruised purple, and the Pacific crashed against the rocks. I was barefoot and letting the salt breeze settle on my skin.

That's when I saw the headlights of a car cut across the driveway. It was a black SUV with tinted windows that rolled to a stop outside my house. My heart raced. I recognized the look immediately, and it was not good.

I poured myself a glass of tequila, stepped onto the porch, and leaned against the doorframe as if nothing could rattle me.

The window rolled down, and I saw a face I hadn't seen in years. It was an old associate and one of the last living links to my old life.

"Ben Skull," he said with syrupy nostalgia. "You're looking good."

"I'm living good," I replied.

He angled his head and smirked. "Are you sure about that?"

His implication was clear to me.

We sat on the patio while the waves kept time. The jokes and banter flowed like old times, but I knew exactly why he had come. I let him speak until he reached his point.

"You know," he began. "A lot of people still respect you. A lot of people still think you're in the game."

I took a slow sip of tequila and set the glass down. "I'm not."

He acted as though he understood and then delivered the pitch. "We have something big coming. It's international, serious money. You would not have to get your hands dirty; all you have to do is connect the right people."

"I'm done," I said in a final tone, shaking my head. "That world is behind me."

He laughed softly. "Nobody's ever done." The way he said those words made me realize in that instant that his visit was not friendly.

His tone changed, and he leaned in until I could see old scar tissue on his temple. "You sure you want to turn this down? Walk away for good? That means no protection, no favors. If somebody comes looking for you, you're on your own."

He let the warning hang between us like it was a final test or a warning. I held his stare. "I don't need protection," I said. "I have God."

A silence settled between us. A breeze moved the palm fronds overhead. Finally, he exhaled through his nose, half amused, half disappointed. "I always knew you were crazy."

He gave me that crooked smirk I remember so well; it was half amusement, half challenge, as if he was sizing me up one last time. Slowly, he finished the last of his drink and then set the glass down. Without a word, he dusted off his hands and slipped back into the SUV. Within moments, the vehicle melted into the shadows of the night and left me alone in the silence.

I stayed outside until the taillights were only a memory. Something inside me felt lighter. It was in that moment that I realized I was finally free. I understood for the first time that freedom does not arrive when other people decide to let you go. Freedom arrives the instant you decide to let them go.

There would be no more proving myself to men who never gave a damn about me. No more debts of any kind. I carried the empty glass inside, found Emily in the kitchen, and kissed her.

"It's really over," I said.

She smiled. It was a knowing smile that tells you someone has been praying for you long before you even thought to pray for yourself.

That night drew a final line between the man I was and the man I am becoming. Now, the past was officially behind me.

The Redemption Build

Chapter 21: Building a New Empire – Skullkrushers

The first time my son Benji said the word "Skullkrushers," I had no idea it would change the course of my life. He was just a Jeep-obsessed five-year-old, and I had just walked in from a meeting with Applbaum, kicking around business ideas with my Mexican attorney 'Little Dirty Taco', who also happened to be my best friend of fifteen years. He was an ex–DA out of San Diego, sharp as hell, fearless, and had stood beside me through some of the most chaotic chapters of my life. We had made money together, smoked more joints than I could count, and he had helped me navigate the fallout from years of damage, including the madness of dealing with my son's mom, who, to put it politely, was one of the worst people I'd ever crossed paths with.

That day, when I got home and asked Benji what a good name would be for a Jeep company, he didn't even hesitate. He just looked at me and said, "Skullkrushers." I stared at him for a second, then practically shouted, "OH YES, BENJI!" That was it.

That was the name. I ran straight to my computer to buy the domain.

Skullcrushers.com was going for $18,000, which was way out of my league at the time. But then I saw *Skullkrushers.com*— with a K—for just $11.99. It was perfect. The "K" made it even better. That was it. The brand was born.

But to understand what that moment meant, you have to go back further... back to a time when I had nothing.

Twenty-two years ago, I had just become a father. My son was born, and I was sleeping on my buddy's couch. I had lost my job after a close friend shut down his firm under SEC heat. I was broke, jobless, and suddenly a father with no plan and backup but just a newborn baby and the weight of knowing I couldn't screw this up.

I started an investor relations firm from scratch and, within thirty days, had closed massive deals, bought a Mercedes, and moved into a three-bedroom apartment by the beach. My life flipped so fast it was dizzying. I didn't just get lucky; I was desperate, and desperation drove me to hustle harder than I ever had before. I believe that moment was the real turning point. Everything that followed—good, bad, insane—can be traced back to the determination born in that first chapter of fatherhood and survival.

***

In my twenties, I had everything I thought I needed or wanted, like money, power, and adrenaline. But I didn't realize then that I was burning out from the inside out, too blinded by the rush to see the wreckage piling up. Fast forward several years, and I had been through the fire, including the Wall Street trades, cartel friend, addiction, relapse, escape, and the endless chase for more. Now, I had finally walked away.

I sold the mansion, left the city, and packed up everything. We moved south, far south, all the way to Cabo San Lucas. There were no more phones ringing off the hook, no Wall Street suits breathing down my neck, and no deals being whispered over cigars and threats. It was just the ocean, the desert, my family, and the sound of a turbocharged off-road rig ripping through the sand. Life slowed down. I finally started breathing again.

Every morning began with the roar of my Jeep kicking up dust. I spent my afternoons with tacos in one hand and an ice-cold beer in the other, watching my kids play while the sun dipped over the Pacific. My wife had her spa days, and my boys and I had our dune runs. For the first time in years, it felt like my life belonged to me again. It was in that stillness, in that space far from Wall Street and all its noise, that the idea for Skullkrushers came to life.

At first, it wasn't much. Just a side hustle, an outlet, something to keep me focused while I figured out what came next. But the more time I spent off-roading, crawling over rocks, tearing through trails, building and modifying Jeeps, the more I realized that people wanted more than just performance. They wanted identity. They wanted grit. They wanted style. Off-roading in Cabo wasn't just a hobby but a way of life. And no one was speaking directly to the renegades, the outcasts, the adrenaline junkies who lived for that thrill. I saw the gap, and I filled it.

When we moved back to San Diego, I hit the ground running. Skullkrushers became my obsession. It was addicting, not like Wall Street or drugs, but a new kind of high. It was pure, relentless determination to turn this brand into a household name. I put Skullkrushers before everything: before sleep, before comfort, even before my own health.

We built it from the garage. I worked fifteen-hour days with no paycheck, pouring every dime from my other businesses back into the brand. Emily was printing 3D gas caps in the garage while pregnant with our son. We were hustling in every sense of the word. I gave everything to build Skullkrushers, not just my time or energy, but my whole heart. I was grinding harder than I ever had on Wall Street, but I'd burned out there chasing money. Now, I was chasing freedom.

I had been through the fire, lost everything, and survived. Now, I wanted to build something that was more than just a business. I wanted something that meant something. Skullkrushers came from the ashes of my past life, but it wasn't just about making money anymore. It was about proving that I could do it the right way. I used everything I had learned from Wall Street, my mafia dealings, from the pain, betrayal, and mistakes, and I poured it all into this new mission. Every lesson became a building block. I surrounded myself with people who believed in the vision. People who cared about growth, grit, and building something worth having.

It wasn't easy. There were nights when I questioned everything. The old habits were still there, whispering in the dark with temptations tugging at my heels. There were days I felt like I was losing the fight and wanted to quit. But then I'd see my wife. I'd hear my kids laugh. And I'd remember that they didn't know the old me. They only knew the man I was trying to become, and I wasn't about to let them down. So, I kept going.

The Jeep community, at first, was full of amazing people: real friendships, real support. It reminded me of the early days on the trading floor. But just like the Street, things shifted. I learned quickly that not everyone clapping for you is rooting for you. I had "friends" start their own Jeep brands right after I brought them in to help me. But there were also a few who became more than friends—our ambassadors, our ride-or-die crew. These weren't just colleagues; they became family. And for them, I would do anything.

Over time, Skullkrushers stopped being just a Jeep company. It became a mindset and a mission! It stood for resilience, grit, and redemption. It was about mental, emotional, and physical strength. It was about never giving up, no matter what the world threw at you. It stood for people who had been through the fire and came out the other side swinging.

And people responded. They saw something real in the brand and its message. The business became a lifestyle. We started selling gear like fitness products, supplements, and clothing, but more importantly, we started building a community. A tribe of people who wanted to live a life that actually meant something.

The turning point came when we partnered with some high-profile athletes who had their own battles to fight. These were the people who saw what I had built and understood it wasn't just about parts but also purpose. Skullkrushers became a symbol of redemption. A badge of honor for anyone who had ever crawled out of a dark place and kept moving forward. We weren't just selling products but were pushing people to be better, stronger, and braver. And the brand exploded. It went viral. Our community grew. Our social media exploded. Our sales went crazy. But the best part wasn't the money. It was the impact. Our name meant something.

That's when I realized this wasn't just my next hustle. This was my real legacy. It wasn't the money I made in the markets or the deals I brokered in the shadows. It wasn't the status or the power I used to chase. This... *this*... was the empire that mattered. Skullkrushers gave me a platform to help people rise, to get stronger, sober, and right. We helped people crush the obstacles in their lives, physically and mentally.

As Skullkrushers grew, I understood something deeper. I had to lose everything to finally create something that would actually matter and make a difference. I wasn't just building a company but a movement.

None of it would have been possible without my wife. She was the foundation, the anchor, the reason I never gave up, even when it felt like everything was crashing down around me. She stood by me through the chaos and never once doubted me. As Skullkrushers grew, I made sure it was built on the values that mattered: integrity, strength, and family. Because I had found that the real treasure wasn't the brand, or the recognition, or even the money. It was the life I was building with the people I loved.

Eight years later, Skullkrushers is on the edge of something huge. We're expanding into the truck market and pushing the brand into places I never imagined. And sometimes, I look at my son Benji and remember the moment he named this dream. He doesn't remember it, but I'll never forget. This company... this legacy... is as much his as it is mine.

Everything I went through, every dollar made, every wrong turn and every night I didn't think I'd make it out alive prepared me for this. The money, the madness, and the moments that nearly broke me all led to this. Skullkrushers is my redemption story. It's proof that you can come back from anything if you've got enough heart and grit. It's been one hell of a ride, and if I've learned anything, it's that the real thrill isn't in the destination— it's in the journey.

And this journey?

It's only just getting started!

Chapter 22: The Accidental Marketing Legend

When Skullkrushers first began, I never imagined I would be at the center of it. I didn't start out wanting to be the CEO or the face of a brand. My plan was simple: invest in a good idea, provide the seed money, and help guide things from the background. I had no desire to be in the spotlight. After everything I'd been through, I was done with attention. I just wanted to build something solid and clean.

As I mentioned earlier, Skullkrushers started in my garage. At the time, I had a partner out in Texas who helped me develop our first inner fender. He was the one handling operations, and I trusted him with that role. I figured I'd play the quiet partner, help fund development, and let him run the show.

But things don't always go the way you plan.

I started noticing my partner's behavior that didn't sit right with me; it was disrespectful, reckless behavior that didn't just reflect poorly on him but on the entire brand we were trying to build. He was sliding into the DMs of married women on

Instagram, acting like a teenage kid in a grown man's body. It was unprofessional and unacceptable. I had already walked away from a life of deception and dirt. I wasn't going to let that energy creep into this new chapter.

So, I had a decision to make: walk away from the business I had just poured ten thousand dollars into—or cut ties and do it on my own.

At the time, that $10,000 was a big deal. I was rebuilding my life, still recovering from years of damage and hard resets. But more than the money, it was about the principle. I had finally found something I cared about, something that felt honest. I wasn't going to let one guy wreck that.

So, I took over. I made the decision that changed everything: I parted ways with my partner and didn't walk away. I was all in. My wife stood beside me in every way while I figured out how to keep the dream alive. It was just the two of us, an idea, and a deep love for building jeep parts. That idea and love were about to become something much bigger.

Building the company wasn't easy. The days were long, the nights even longer, and nothing was guaranteed. There were no shortcuts. Just grit, hope and hours in the garage turning parts into a business. I had no employees, no marketing team, and no roadmap. But I had something better: purpose. Slowly, piece by piece, we expanded from a garage operation to two full-blown production facilities shipping worldwide. Our custom Jeep fenders caught on first, and before long, we were breaking into the truck and Can-Am markets too.

But none of that could've prepared me for the marketing moment that would turn everything on its head in the history of Skullkrushers, and it happened entirely by accident!

In 2017, I decided to make my first major road trip from San Diego to Daytona Beach for a show, hauling a jeep behind me. It was a big move for the brand. We were finally starting to grow, and I wanted to show up strong. There was only one problem: I had never towed anything in my life. Not a single vehicle. But I figured, how hard could it be?

The trip started fine. But by the time I reached Arizona, it was past midnight. I was running on fumes, having no sleep, stiff muscles, and a truck that felt like an oven during the day and a freezer at night. I pulled into a hotel parking lot to get a few hours of rest. It had a covered structure, but I was too tired and sleepy to think straight. Thus, I didn't even think twice and just drove in.

And that's when it happened.

BAM!

There was a loud crash and a violent lurch. A thunderous crunch echoed through the parking lot. Suddenly, my truck was up on two wheels!

I had completely miscalculated the height. The Jeep on my trailer was too tall, and the roof rack had slammed into the overhead structure, ripping the hardtop clean off. Fiberglass and glass were everywhere. I stood there in the middle of the night, freezing and exhausted, staring at the mess I'd just made. The hardtop weighed close to 300 pounds. My hands were already torn up from working all day, but I couldn't leave that Jeep top sitting in plain sight. I had to get it out of there.

Adrenaline kicked in. I somehow hoisted that beast of a hardtop, still attached to the rack, and with an insane burst of energy, hurled it over a nearby balcony into the bushes. My hands got cut by fiberglass, and it tore up my arms and wrecked my back, but I got it done; the evidence was hidden.

Bleeding, dirty and barely able to stand, I stumbled into the hotel. The guy at the front desk didn't ask questions. He just handed me a box of Band-Aids and gave me a look like, "What the hell happened to you?"

The next morning, I had another choice to make: pack it up and go home or push through. I woke up in pain from head to toe. My abs were on fire, my back was shot, and all I had were four ibuprofen. But quitting wasn't an option. I found the hardtop where I had tossed it, jumped the railing, and somehow lifted that 300-pound beast back up onto my scratched-to-hell truck. Then I hit the road again.

What I didn't expect was the response.

I had been posting the whole saga on Facebook and Instagram as it happened—part venting, part entertainment. People watched it all unfold in real-time. They laughed, cringed, and rooted for me. By the time I arrived in Daytona, people already knew the story. "You're the guy who ripped the top off his Jeep!" they said.

Crowds were lining up at our booth, not just for the products but to hear the full story. They wanted to take photos and ask questions because I think they didn't just see a brand. They saw someone who had gone through hell to chase something he believed in.

That trip turned out to be the best accidental marketing campaign I ever launched.

That year, Skullkrushers exploded. Sales skyrocketed. Our social media numbers jumped. Although people were buying Jeep parts, I think more than that, they were buying the story. They were buying authenticity. They were buying the struggle behind it. In hindsight, it was a disaster, and I wouldn't wish it on anyone, but who knew it would be a source of such success for our business?

It turns out people don't always connect with a polished brand or perfect marketing. They connect with the real... with the struggle... with the guy who bleeds for his dream and still keeps going. They want to see the blood, sweat, and failure behind the success. They want to know the person behind the product. That trip probably taught me more about branding than any book, ad campaign, or agency ever could.

And yeah, to this day, my back still hurts from that night. Between that and the time I drove a BMW through a roof, I'm probably carrying a chiropractor's retirement plan in my spine. But you know what? I'd do it all over again. Because that trip didn't just mark a turning point for the business, it became part of the Skullkrushers' story. And, like many things in my life, it wasn't pretty. But it was real. And it worked!

Chapter 23: The Legacy Play

I thought I was done with Wall Street for good. After everything I'd been through, I had finally found peace building Skullkrushers. For the first time in years, I was living clean, focused, and free.

But life has a way of circling back, sometimes when you least expect it.

It was about three years ago when I found myself stepping back into the world I thought I'd left behind for good. The return wasn't flashy. There was no big announcement or triumphant homecoming. It started with a phone call from a man I'll call **H**.

H wasn't just anyone. He was my best friend of 25 years—a guy I've trusted through thick and thin. We'd seen each other through the chaos, the hustle, the heartbreak, and the healing. We'd done business together back then and had always been best friends in the game. He was the kind of guy who did everything by the book, never cutting corners. One day, he called me out of the blue and said, "Benny, you ready to get back in the game?" Just like that, I found a home, a place of love in the Beehive State, where I could grow in the finance business, spread my wings, and make a grand re-entrance on Wall Street, this time on my terms.

It hit different. This wasn't just another job offer. It was a door opening to something more grounded, more aligned with who I had become. What he offered me was salary and more importantly trust. And this family office wasn't like the places I worked when I was younger. There was no backdoor dealing, no whispers of corruption, no bending the rules to get ahead. This place was built on values and that mattered to me.

I had been texting H every single week for nearly five years, asking if there was a spot on his team. While I was deep in the grind building Skullkrushers, trying to provide for my family and keep the wheels turning, I knew that if any person could show me the next step in finance, it was him.

For almost five years, I sent those messages. Week after week, no pressure—just persistence. Then one day, H finally called me back. His voice on the other end was calm and clear: "I got a spot for you. Salary's there. Come join the team."

And just like that, I was back in.

But this time, it wasn't investor relations like before. H brought me into a different lane: the lending side of the business. Loans, underwriting, structuring deals... it was a whole new game. And I dove into it headfirst. Our team specialized in non-recourse stock loans, working with shareholders, investors, CEOs, and executives.

G, one of H's guys trained me every day for three years— never leaving my side, pushing me to become a better businessman, and getting my fitness game back on point. G was a former drug addict who had been sober for 10 years and had turned into an absolute stud—a straight-up fitness beast and a good-looking SOB. He had it all, and I grew to respect both him and H.

H had been building this company since 2005, carrying it on his back. He had the best name on Wall Street—and in that world, your name is everything—even while swimming with sharks.

G and H actually had my back, for the first real time in my life, I felt like I was part of a team. H's rules were simple: "Do as you say, and say as you do"—at any cost.

For the past three years, I've been rebuilding my book of business, this time from the loan side of the fence. I had to learn fast, adapt faster, and lean on everything I'd learned from Wall Street, Skullkrushers, and the fires I'd survived. The hustle, the discipline, the relationships—they all translated. But now, I was playing a cleaner game, with a clearer mind, and with people I actually trusted. I embraced it the same way I had embraced every chapter of my life: with hunger, curiosity, and a refusal to be outworked.

***

Back on Wall Street, the game hadn't changed, but I had. I wasn't chasing quick wins or trying to prove anything. I was building something that could stand the test of time. The energy was still there, but what fueled me wasn't the rush of daily trades or the chase for the next big score. It was the bigger picture.

We had made a quiet but powerful promise to ourselves, to our clients, and to everyone who believed in us that we would do it differently. No shortcuts. No smoke and mirrors. I had already lived through the world of quick wins and high-stakes risks. I knew the cost. I had seen how easy it was to get lost in the noise and lose sight of things.

This time, we were focused on building something with strong roots. We set out to build a business model that wouldn't just ride the waves of the market, but outlast them. Every client we worked with, every deal we made, and every partnership we formed was based on trust and honesty. We didn't have to cheat, trick, or take shortcuts to succeed. My mission was simple: build a firm on integrity, not illusion.

Every decision was rooted in core values:

1. Put the client first, always.
2. Be honest and tell the truth, even when it's hard.
3. Think long-term, not short-term.
4. Lead with ethics, not ego.

We only brought in people who shared that vision and wanted to win but also wanted to do it right. Accountability became the backbone of our culture, where every win was earned, and every mistake became a lesson. Every person on the team knew their role mattered and that we were all holding each other to the highest bar.

While we respected traditional values, we weren't stuck in the past. The world was changing fast. Technology and data were transforming the financial industry, and we welcomed those changes. Data, automation, and artificial intelligence were rewriting the playbook. If we wanted to lead, we couldn't just adapt but had to anticipate.

We invested heavily in cutting-edge tools and analytics, but we never forgot the human side of the business. Algorithms could process data. But only experience could read between the lines. We tried to stay ahead of the curve by balancing both.

Tech gave us an edge, but it was still experience and instinct that made the difference. Our goal wasn't to follow the market but to lead it. We didn't want to just respond to changes after they happened but wanted to stay ahead of them. Our goal was to be proactive, always thinking ahead, spotting what was coming next, and being ready before anyone else. That's how we stayed one step ahead in a fast-moving world.

As the business gained momentum, I found myself thinking deeply about what truly mattered. At first, it was easy to focus on numbers, such as the size of the portfolios, the speed of the trades, or the steady climb of performance charts. But over time, something became very clear: the real value of what we were building wasn't measured in spreadsheets or stock tickers.

It was in the people.

The most meaningful part of our growth came from the trust our clients placed in us, the honest conversations, and the partnerships that felt more like friendships. Those relationships became the foundation of everything. They brought purpose to the work and gave it a human side that numbers alone could never provide.

Our clients weren't just numbers but real people; they were parents saving for their kids' futures, retirees looking for peace of mind, entrepreneurs betting on themselves. We listened, we learned, and we built personalized strategies to help them win.

We took the time to understand them, to listen, and to craft strategies tailored to their lives. That's why they stayed with us. It wasn't just about commissions. It was about connection. And that's what brought them back, year after year.

***

Success in the market was great, but I wanted something deeper. When I looked back, I didn't want my legacy to be a list of big trades or dollar signs. I didn't get into this business to be famous. I got in to prove something to myself and to the world. But in the end, it wasn't the size of the deals that mattered. It was the *way* I did them. I wanted to be remembered for standing tall when it would've been easier to take shortcuts.

Our firm became a beacon in an industry often ruled by deception. I wanted to walk away from this industry with my integrity intact. And I did. I built a firm that people respected.

Eventually, I realized this wasn't just about us. We were laying the groundwork for the next generation. I didn't want young entrepreneurs and traders to learn the hard way like I did. I wanted to guide them.

***

The future seems bright.

We've built something with strong, deep, and steady roots. It stands strong in any market because it was built on truth, not trends. But we're just getting started.

We'll keep pushing boundaries. We'll keep innovating. We'll keep choosing people over profit, and principle over popularity.

Because the man I used to be? He lived for the thrill.

But the man I've become? He lives for the legacy.

Chapter 24: Looking Back to Move Forward

They say when a man falls hard enough, he either stays down or rises as someone new. Me? I fell a hundred times over before I figured out how to live.

Let me take you back for a second—not to the money, the cars, or the chaos. That part of the story's been told. What hasn't been said loud enough is what happened after I lost everything. The nights when the silence was louder than any party I'd ever thrown. The mornings when I woke up, not knowing who I was without the Wall Street swagger or the fear factor. That man you read about in the early chapters, who thought he was untouchable? He's gone.

What's left is what mattered all along.

No one warns you how quiet it gets when the phones stop ringing. When the "boys" vanish, when the so-called brothers-in-arms suddenly forget your number, when the world that once begged to be in your presence moves on without a blink.

At first, I tried to fight it. Took another trip. Plotted another deal. I couldn't accept that it was over. But one night, I was alone and angry, staring into the black void above me. I realized I wasn't mourning the loss of wealth. I was mourning the man I had become: ruthless, empty and paranoid. I had built an empire with fast cash and thought I could buy peace with quick money.

Spoiler alert: you can't.

I've had time now—time to breathe, to step back, and to really look at my life. And as crazy as it sounds, after everything I've been through, I wouldn't take any of it back. Not a single damn second.

Because the man I've become? He was forged in that fire. Every sleepless night in Panama, every handshake, every Wall Street brawl, every courtroom, crisis, and collapse—it was all part of the story. At the time, I didn't know it. I thought I was invincible. I thought I was writing the rulebook. But in reality, life was schooling me. Those years of wild living weren't just about chasing adrenaline or stacking cash. They were lessons... brutal, expensive, soul-wrecking lessons.

If there's one thing I learned the hard way, it's this: money, power, and fame are hollow prizes when you're empty inside. They'll make you feel important for a while. They'll give you the illusion of control. But in the quiet moments, when the lights are off and the world isn't watching, you'll realize that none of it matters if your soul is bankrupt.

The real currency in this life? Family. Faith. Integrity.

You can fake a lot of things in life. Loyalty, confidence, even love, but you can't fake what the mirror tells you. And when I finally faced it, really faced it, I saw a man who had run out of excuses. I wasn't just broke financially. I was morally bankrupt.

And yet... that's when it started to shift.

Funny how life works. When the noise faded and the yes-men disappeared, all that remained was me and a whisper that asked, 'Are you done pretending?'

Let me be clear: redemption isn't some poetic walk into the sunrise. It's messy, it's slow, and it damn well hurts! Every step I took toward rebuilding meant owning the wreckage I left behind. Swallowing my pride in front of my wife. Letting my kids see the cracks in their so-called hero.

But here's the thing: the more real I got, the more freedom I felt.

Turns out, the bravest thing I ever did wasn't flipping a stock in the middle of a crash or walking into a meeting without flinching. It was telling the truth.

When the walls caved in, I expected no one to be there. But she was. My wife. The woman who had every reason to leave, every right to slam the door. She stayed. A few friends did too. And my kids? They didn't need a king. They just needed a dad who showed up.

That's when I realized I didn't lose everything. I had my core. The real ones. The people who didn't care about how many zeros were in my bank account. They cared about whether I could be present. And that, my friend, became my new currency.

***

Back then, I only believed in one thing: myself. I was deep in the life, high on control, foolishly thinking I was untouchable. But in reality, I was just riding chaos, chasing power, with no direction and no anchor.

When it all collapsed, I was stripped bare. It was just me and the wreckage. That was the moment I had to face what I'd become.

But rock bottom has a way of clearing the fog. It's where I first began to believe in faith and in the raw power of change, redemption and second chances.

Letting go of control was the turning point. Once I surrendered that grip, things began to fall into place—not perfectly or instantly, but with purpose.

***

I've always believed in the power of manifestation, but not in the new-age, crystal-gazing, wish-upon-a-star way people talk about these days. For me, manifestation has always meant this: faith in God, faith in hard work, and faith in the unshakable belief that what I seek is already mine.

Because if you're not willing to sweat for your vision, it stays a fantasy. Every major milestone in my life—the cars I've driven, the homes I've lived in, the woman I married—was the result of a vision I held with relentless belief. But here's what I believe in: manifestation without action is just daydreaming. You don't get anywhere by sitting back and hoping. You have to move with intention.

When I was a kid in England, drifting through foster homes, luxury cars were more like UFOs than actual vehicles to me. I was obsessed with exotic cars. Nobody around me drove

Porsches or lifted trucks that roared like monsters. That was a different world… another planet for me.

But in my mind, I saw them. In the dark, broken corners of my childhood, those cars became symbols of freedom, power and escape. And even when I was a broke teenager scraping by in California, I'd whisper to myself: *One day, I'll drive whatever the hell I want.*

I didn't know how, and I didn't care. I didn't know the route—I just knew I was working toward a place I wanted to be. I worked like the keys were already in my hands.

Wall Street. Skullkrushers. Every hustle I put my name on, I went all in. I visualized those beasts parked in my garage before they ever existed in my reality. I felt the steering wheel before I touched it. I heard the engine before I bought it.

And sure enough, one by one, the cars came rolling in. Aston Martin. Range Rovers. Mercedes. Jeeps. Porsches. Custom trucks that turned freeways into runways. Some people called it luck. But it wasn't just luck or hustle. Every time I got behind the wheel of one of those cars, I felt like I had manifested it with God's help.

And the same way I envisioned those cars, those homes, those milestones, I envisioned her. Long before I met my wife, I knew her, not by name or face but by presence. I had this clear, stubborn image of the woman I needed by my side. A warrior... A partner... A queen who wouldn't flinch at my past or fold under the weight of my future. She wasn't going to be soft-spoken or easily impressed. She wouldn't sugarcoat the truth or tiptoe around my demons—she would face them head-on, refusing to let me fall into comfort or complacency. I wasn't looking for someone to complete me; I was preparing for someone who could stand beside me, fully formed, fully aware, and fully ready.

So I worked. I prepared for her the way you prepare for battle—with discipline, intention, and prayer. I sharpened myself and became the kind of man who wouldn't just attract her, but who could actually keep her.

And then, she arrived. There was no cinematic moment, no dramatic music or picture-perfect introduction. But the moment she walked into my life, I recognized her immediately—not because she fit a checklist, but because she matched the vision I had carried for so long.

She was more than what I hoped for. And just like the cars and the homes I had manifested before, I knew without a doubt: this was it. She was the blessing I had been preparing for. I feel like that's the real essence of manifestation. It's not just about visualizing the life you want but becoming ready to receive it. If

I hadn't been prepared for a woman like her, I could have missed her completely.

I've lived everywhere. Couches. Rooms. Cramped rentals. A beach shack or two. But even in my lowest seasons, I was walking through mansions in my mind.

That's the thing about real manifestation—it's not something you see outside of you first. It's something you hold inside, long before the world catches up.

Every home I've ever owned? I walked through it in my imagination first. I saw the floors. The kitchen. The way the sun hit the driveway. I would close my eyes and feel the doorknob in my palm like it already belonged to me.

When I bought my first real house, the one that felt like a "win," not just a roof, I wasn't surprised. I had already lived there a hundred times in my head. I had already prayed over those walls, thanked God for that door before I had the key in my hand. By the time I signed the paperwork, the house felt familiar. It felt earned. It felt like something I had already owned.

From fixer-uppers to beachfront houses, every property was already mine long before the ink hit the deed. That's the kind of faith I'm talking about—not wishful thinking, but confident certainty.

Every property I've owned since then has followed that same pattern. I never chased after them blindly. I never doubted. I trusted that if the vision was there, the blessing would be too. Even if it wasn't on the market yet, even if people told me I couldn't afford it, I believed it was mine.

A lot of people like to talk about manifestation these days, like it's a magic trick. Sometimes people ask me all the time if I believe in manifestation. My answer? *Only if you understand what it really is.*

Manifestation is not magic or a spell. It's faith in motion. Every blessing I've received didn't land in my lap because I hoped for them. They came because I prayed for them and trained like it. Moved like it. Sacrificed like it.

In my opinion, the difference between winning and watching others win is the mindset. Most people lose the battle before they even start. Doubt creeps in, or insecurity takes over. They tell themselves it's not possible, or worse, they listen to the people who tell them they're not worthy.

But I never gave that voice a seat at my table. If there was a vision in my mind, then I believed it was already mine. That's the truth nobody talks about: You have to move like it's yours before it ever is. That's how you turn a prayer into a paycheck, a vision into a legacy.

That's how I built this life, from the ground up, from nothing but grit, prayer and a fire inside my heart that refused to go out.

***

People talk about legacy like it's something you leave behind when you die. But I've come to learn that legacy is something you live every single day.

It's not about the bank account. It's not about the house on the hill or the cars in the driveway. Legacy is about impact, values and what people say about you when you're not in the room.

My kids won't grow up remembering the man I used to be. They'll know the man I chose to become. And that's everything to me.

That's why I built Skullkrushers. Not just to create another business, but to create a movement... A brotherhood... A second chance. We built a community—a place for people with pasts, with scars, for those who've fallen and are ready to rise again. Skullkrushers isn't just about the fight in the market—it's about the fight in life. It's about refusing to be defined by your worst mistake. We help people smash through their old narratives and build something real and honorable. That's legacy to me.

***

This isn't the end of the story. It's just the beginning. I'm not done growing, learning, or serving. The difference now is that I'm no longer running or hiding behind wealth or ego or reputation.

Now it's about showing up with clarity, walking with purpose, and doing the work in business, in family, and within myself. I wake up every day with a renewed sense of mission. Not to prove something to the world, but to honor the second chance I've been given.

When I think about where I started—abandoned, angry, bouncing through foster homes—and where I landed... it still takes my breath away for a moment. This ride has been anything but easy.

But every chapter mattered. Because the ultimate lesson is this: *Your past doesn't define you. Your choices do.* It doesn't matter how far you've fallen, how deep the hole is, or how many times you've screwed up. If you're willing to take ownership and fight, you can build something beautiful out of the wreckage.

I did. And if I can do it, so can you.

And if you've made it this far—if you're reading this, wondering whether your past disqualifies you, or if your life feels like one giant mistake—I want you to hear this loud and clear:

You are not done.

You are not finished.

You are not broken beyond repair.

So, stand up. Dust off. Build your own version of Skullkrushers. Whatever it looks like. Whatever it takes.

My message to you, from one survivor to another:

Rise. Never quit!

Chapter 25: A New Beginning.

Life has a funny way of coming full circle.

If you had told me years ago, when I was deep in the madness of Wall Street, buried in trades, risk, and shadows, that I'd one day get the opportunity to live in Utah with my wife and five boys, building something clean, I probably would've laughed. Or maybe just lit a cigar and changed the subject.

But here I am.

After everything I've lived—fast money, harder losses, Skullkrushers—I'm back in the market. But this time, I'm not playing the same game. This time, it's on my terms.

And I wouldn't shy from saying that it's 100% clean.

I'm part of a firm made up of hard-working men who do it the right way. No gimmicks. No lies. Just hustle, discipline, and relentless focus. What makes it even more powerful is that most of the guys I work with weren't born with polished resumes or silver spoons. Some were heroin addicts. Some had rap sheets. Some had completely lost their way. But they turned it around.

They cleaned up, fought like hell to reclaim their lives, and now show up sharper, stronger, and more focused than most of the guys I ever worked with in a suit. They know what it means to hit rock bottom and more importantly, they know what it means to climb back.

That kind of resilience? I don't think you can fake it.

These aren't Wall Street robots chasing zeros. These are men with scars, purpose, and a fire that doesn't go out when things get hard. And so, the firm we've built together is not just respected but also feared in the right way. We're not here to play small. But we're also not playing dirty. We're here to do it right. And win.

Now my firm is based out of Utah, and I'm up there about once a month, working alongside some of the best people in the business. My buddy G, who trained me, is one of them—he was a former addict, and now he's absolutely taking the world by storm. It's powerful to see a young guy fully stepping into his potential.

And then there's my boy H. He gave me a shot at this firm in Salt Lake City when I needed it most. He and his partner were 50/50 on me—my past was wild, and they knew it. But they still took a chance. I'm forever grateful they did. Because the truth is, that crazy past humbled me. And spending the last eight years broke, grinding to build Skullkrushers from the dirt up—that was all part of God's plan. That struggle was meant to shape me.

Now, with everything finally lining up and the money starting to come back around, I'm more grounded than I've ever been. Humbled, focused, and ready. Every part of that journey mattered.

We're even looking at property out there now—trying to move the family to Utah and finally get out of the hood in SoCal. It's time for peace, space, and a fresh chapter. And it feels like everything is falling into place just how it's supposed to.

We're building something rooted in values, not shortcuts. Something you can be proud of. Something your kids can look up to. It's refreshing, to say the least.

So this summer, my family and I would make the move to Utah. It might not be the flashiest move I've made, but it might be the most important.

We've lived in so many places, including San Diego, Cabo, and Nicaragua. We've seen palm trees and police tape, paradise and pressure, beach views and broken dreams. We've survived every storm together. And now, finally, we get to plant roots in a place that's stable, quiet, focused and forward-facing.

For years, we lived in the shadows of Southern California's gritty streets. Sure, we had made money but it came with noise. The kind of noise that sticks to your skin and reminds you of everything you're trying to leave behind. The surroundings still echoed with reminders of who I used to be. It didn't feel like home anymore but rather a trapdoor back to a life I had fought hard to escape.

And I ain't going back.

We've outgrown that space. My wife deserves better. My sons deserve better. And I am finally ready to build better.

So, we'll be packing up our lives and heading to Salt Lake City, Utah, the new home of our family office and the foundation for our future.

***

You might question, *Why Salt Lake City?*

Well, because it represents everything I'm building toward now. Peace. Progress. Purpose.

It seems like a city with a mindset. A clean break. A symbolic shift from everything I used to chase toward everything I now want to build. The business scene is growing. The energy is optimistic. And the distractions are gone. No old habits lurking around the corner. No ghosts of the man I used to be. Just space to grow, think clearly, and lay down roots that will last for generations.

Salt Lake gives me the environment I need to think long-term—not just in business, but in life. I don't just want success anymore... I want **legacy**. I want my boys to grow up seeing what real leadership looks like. I want them to understand that strength isn't about power but about doing what's right when no one's watching.

That's the world we're building now.

The house, the office, and the mission are all being redefined here. Not as an escape, but as an elevation. Not as a retreat, but a recalibration. We're still grinding and growing. But we're doing it on solid ground, with clear minds and clean hearts.

***

Now, as I sit in my office overlooking this new chapter, I can't help but reflect. I've spent so much of my life chasing the next big thing: money, adrenaline, danger, reputation and sometimes every one of these things simultaneously. And don't get me wrong, I learned a lot. I paid my dues. But the real prize wasn't in the chase.

It's in the people you build with, the integrity you maintain and the legacy you leave behind.

I really believe that this isn't the end. Not by a long shot. But it feels like a beautiful ending to one book, and the powerful beginning of another.

A new city...

A new mission...

A new beginning...

This time, I hope it's built to last.